PIECES OF *Us*

DEDICATION

For Rod Serling

for inspiring generations of
storytellers by unlocking doors with
the key of imagination

PIECES OF *Us*

THE MAKING OF JORDAN PEELE'S MODERN HORROR CLASSIC

WRITTEN BY
CASEEN GAINES

INSIGHT EDITIONS
SAN RAFAEL • LOS ANGELES • LONDON

CONTENTS

PROLOGUE
They've Been Planning This *9*

CHAPTER 1
A Chain of Good Samaritans *13*

CHAPTER 2
Whac-a-Mole *19*

CHAPTER 3
Find Yourself *31*

CHAPTER 4
Three Pointing Back at You *39*

CHAPTER 5
5 On It *55*

CHAPTER 6
Just An Itsy-Bitsy Thing *63*

CHAPTER 7
We're Americans *71*

CHAPTER 8
She Wasn't a Reflection *87*

CHAPTER 9
Good Vibrations *93*

CHAPTER 10
If It Weren't for You *101*

EPILOGUE
It's Us *119*

Acknowledgments *128*

FOLLOWING SPREAD: Jordan Peele and Lupita Nyong'o pose alongside the Merlin's Forest façade.

MERLIN'S
FIND
YOU MUST BE THIS TALL TO ENTER

FOREST
IR SELF

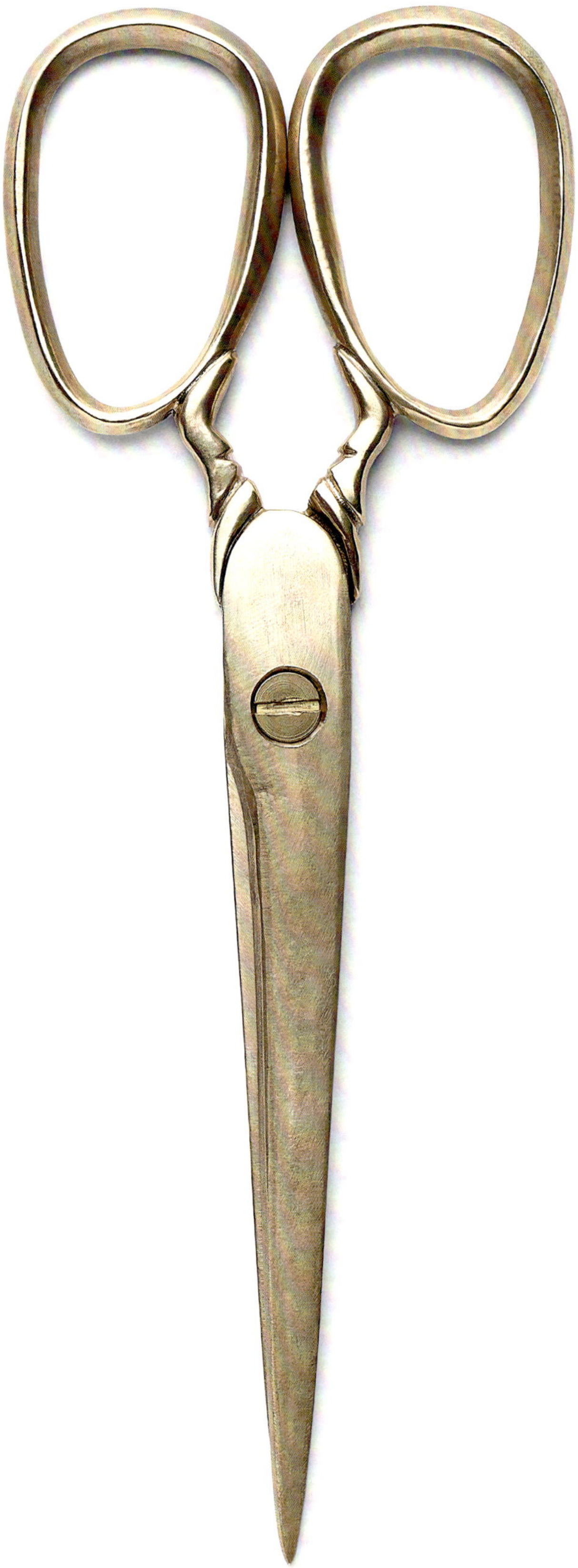

PROLOGUE

THEY'VE BEEN PLANNING THIS

While in search for a new nightmare, Jordan Peele's mind recalled an old one. The memory arrived in the form of a 1960 episode of the classic television series *The Twilight Zone*, wherein a woman at a bus stop—played by Vera Miles, who costarred in Alfred Hitchcock's *Psycho* that same year—sees the physical embodiment of herself. The episode, "Mirror Image," led to one of Peele's earliest haunting experiences. "I've been terrified of the idea of doppelgängers since I was a kid," he says. "I always had this vision of seeing myself across the subway platform and just thought, 'What if you saw yourself?'—and then, if that's not creepy enough, 'What if the other 'you' sort of smiled at you?'"

The imagined experience left an impression on Peele. When the writer-director was thinking of an idea to follow up his critically and commercially successful debut, the Academy Award–winning 2017 film *Get Out*, he ran toward what scared him most. "The idea for this movie came from a deep-seated fear in doppelgängers," he says. "I love the doppelgänger mythologies and different movies that have dealt with them, and I just desperately wanted to make my offering to that pantheon of 'evil double' films."

As a lifelong horror-movie fan, Peele was familiar with cinema's longstanding history of using doubles as a vehicle for scary storytelling—and for conveying a message. For example, Don Siegel's 1956 thriller *Invasion of the Body Snatchers*, which centers on an extraterrestrial invasion of emotionless "pod people" who replicate the physical attributes, memories, and personalities of humans, is viewed by many critics as a commentary on anti-individualism. At the time of the film's release, the United States was in the midst of McCarthyism, a movement of political repression that resulted in a Cold War–era witch hunt that caused Americans to fear and, in many cases, falsely accuse, their neighbors. In both *Body Snatchers* and in real life, the enemy could be anywhere, as even the most banal person could be masking a dark secret.

OPPOSITE: A pair of gold scissors, the fatal weapon of the Tethered.
ABOVE: Slating the home invasion scene.

While cinematic doppelgängers have had a long history, from 1920's *Dr. Jekyll and Mr. Hyde* to 2010's *Black Swan* and beyond, what excited Jordan Peele most was putting his unique spin on the idea. He saw his new film, *Us*, as an opportunity to use duality as a device to comment on the United States' increasingly divided society.

If *Get Out* is considered to be written in response to the widespread notion that Barack Obama's presidency had moved America into a "postracial" era, it could be argued that *Us* was Peele's allegorical reaction to the first Donald Trump administration. The story comes out of the shift in the United States' political and social discourse, particularly as it pertained to increasingly inflammatory rhetoric and fears of immigrants and individuals from other historically marginalized communities.

"I think that this movie applies in any version of 'us versus them,'" Peele says, "whether we're talking on the level of your family versus the family across the street, your race versus another race, your socioeconomic class versus another, or the idea of us being Americans against the rest of the world. I think we are conditioned to point the finger at 'them.' This movie says we need to point the finger at ourselves, at us. We are often our own worst enemy."

"This film is operating on multiple levels," Ian Cooper, Peele's producing partner and longtime friend, says. "It's about how the things we think we've gotten away with come back to haunt us. And beneath that, it's about how, in American culture, we often claim that 'the other,' some group outside of ourselves, is the problem. With this script, Jordan has given us an 'other' that is a terrifying force to be reckoned with, and it is ourselves."

Peele's concept evolved into a story centered on the Wilsons, an all-American Black family, who are attacked by their doppelgängers, the Tethered. The film follows Adelaide, the family's matriarch, who, the audience is shown, experienced a disturbing incident as a child and is attempting to move beyond, and mask, that experience. "Now she has kids and a husband, the perfect American family," Peele says. "But that trauma is still lingering in her subconscious, at the very least, and at the most in her conscious [mind]. As she comes back with her family to the house she grew up in, which is now their summer house, she's returning to the location of her original trauma and she starts to sense that something is wrong."

Santa Cruz, a coastal city in California, emerged as the ideal backdrop for Peele's story. The writer-director was drawn to juxtaposing the town's tourist-filled Boardwalk, replete with amusement park rides and carnival-style games, with a horrific story, drawing inspiration from Alfred Hitchcock films like *The Birds* and *Vertigo*—the latter also featuring a doppelgänger—but dialing up the contrast to new heights. "I love the idea of subverting really idyllic locations," Peele says. "I love giving the audience a vacation in the middle of the horror, if I can."

With an idea fleshed out into a screenplay, Peele began assembling a team to bring his vision to reality. One of the first people brought into the fold was storyboard artist Eric Yamamoto, who Peele had previously collaborated with on *Get Out*.

"I read the script and was starting to see the connections," Yamamoto says. "It wasn't just *Us*—it was *US*, the United States—and I thought that was interesting."

ABOVE: Lupita Nyong'o sheds a single tear as Red.

“The doppelgänger idea connected with me as an artist, because we are our own worst critics,” he says. “We are our own worst enemy.”

“I think about . . . why seeing yourself is so scary,” Peele says. “No one really wants to look at their faults, their guilt, their demons. We want to look elsewhere.”

Production designer Ruth De Jong was another key member of the creative team, tasked with overseeing every aesthetic aspect of production. “We’re a great pair,” she says, referring to her relationship with Peele. “He’s writing with his audience in mind, and I am designing with his story in mind.

“He had seen two things I had previously done,” De Jong adds. “*Manchester by the Sea* was a very tiny indie, and it was so grounded in real life, but *Twin Peaks* (2017) is the artistry of David Lynch and these other worlds—and I think Jordan wants both. He wants his stories to be incredibly tangible and grounded, but he also wants these altered states.”

“The key elements of a Jordan Peele film are innovation, terror, mischief, and iconic imagery,” producer Ian Cooper says.

“The details make a story,” Peele says. “Specificity tethers an audience to a reality they recognize. With attention to the particulars, you can ground the biggest and craziest ideas.”

With *Get Out*, Peele established himself as an austere filmmaker with a sharp eye for visual storytelling. *Us* pushed his skills to the next level. Attention was paid to every detail, with the result being simultaneously haunting and thought-provoking.

“Collaborating with Jordan is truly incredible,” De Jong says. “He’s so open and approachable, and that makes for a fluid relationship and very productive conversations. His script is his bible, but he’s constantly rewriting and thinking of ideas. There’s this constant dialogue between him and the art department and props and set decoration. It’s organic, and fluid, and wonderful.”

“It’s an incredible experience to work with somebody who’s so focused and confident in what he wants,” she continues. “I can’t say enough beautiful things about him.”

In *Us*, Peele and his creative team paid great attention to every detail. “Jordan writes in a very layered fashion, and he writes with symbolism,” Lupita Nyong’o says. “Things aren’t what they seem.”

“This is a movie that keeps revealing itself to the audience,” Ian Cooper says. “We keep peeling back these layers, so the audience never really knows what’s coming, even if they think they do.”

Throughout *Us*, Peele encourages his audience to look beyond the surface. This book is one guide down the rabbit hole.

ABOVE: Lupita Nyong’o, as Adelaide, studies a photo of herself as a child.

HANDSACROSSAMERICA
1986

CHAPTER 1

A CHAIN OF GOOD SAMARITANS

From the very first moment of *Us*, Peele subverts audience expectations. We hear the sound of waves crashing against the shoreline as the Universal Pictures logo fills the screen, continuing while an epigraph appears onscreen: "There are thousands of miles of tunnels beneath the continental United States . . . Abandoned subway systems, unused service routes, and deserted mine shafts . . . Many have no known purpose at all." Each line dissipates in sequence, as if washed away by the sea we've been hearing.

The sounds of waves should convey tranquility, but in this case, it's foreboding. This is confirmed when the film's first image is revealed. It is 1986, and we are in a sitting room. Peele keeps his camera transfixed on a television set airing an evening-news weather report.

The sounds we've been hearing aren't gentle waves. A thunderstorm is imminent, and the image on the screen—two lightning bolts emanating from two thunderclouds, each with two arrows pointing toward Santa Cruz on the crude illustrated map of the California coast—establishes the theme of duality, while confirming that something bad is afoot.

The television is surrounded by shelves, flanked with VHS cassette tapes of films that, within the context of *Us*, will influence the planning, the garments, the weapons, and the vision for the doppelgängers' eventual attempted takeover.

OPPOSITE: Young Addy's Hands Across America shirt.
ABOVE: The Wilson sitting room television set circa 1986.

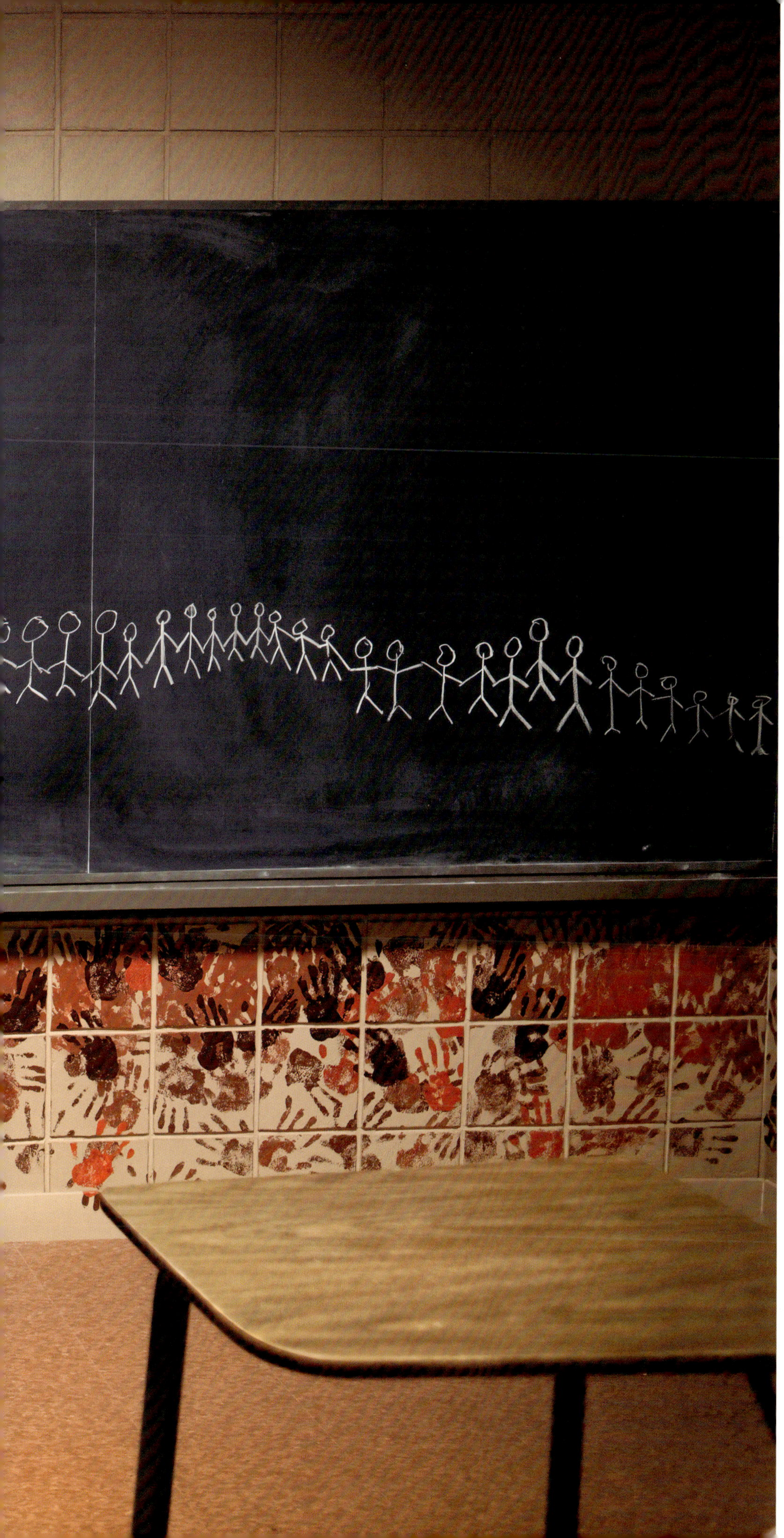

"Starting with this opening shot of the Hands Across America commercial and having audiences watch alongside young Addy was important to establish her key influences, to Addy's future expression, as well as to lead audiences to trust her. And as we find out, of course, that ultimate form of expression is leading the Tethered based on these images she recalls from her youth."

—JORDAN PEELE

Outside of the narrative, these cassettes provide a road map to some of Peele's influences as a filmmaker:

- *The Man with Two Brains* (1983) is a dark comedy wherein a scientist played by Steve Martin falls in love with a talking brain. According to Peele, the movie is significant to his cinematic universe on two fronts: It is a thematic reference to *Us*—"The idea of two intelligences sharing a soul," Peele says—and a reference to *Get Out*, wherein white brains are transplanted into unwilling Black bodies.

- *The Goonies* (1985) is a coming-of-age adventure centered on young children who find a hidden world through underground tunnels. For Peele, the film's significance extends to the legacy of its stars. "Corey Feldman [is] a very important figure for our generation," he says. "And [Corey] Haim too . . . . They were kids who were as cool as it got. And stories of great duality, sagas of the greatest highs and the lowest lows."

- *C.H.U.D.* (1984)—the title of which stands for "cannibalistic humanoid underground dwellers"—is based in New York City, where mutant "undergrounders" emerge from the sewers.

- *The Right Stuff* (1983) is an Academy Award–winning historical drama following a group of US military test pilots selected to participate in the first manned flights into outer space. In a literal sense, it is a story of upward conquest. Like the Tethered, the doppelgängers in *Us* who live underground, the astronauts are stated in the film as going "higher, farther, and faster than any other American."

- *A Nightmare on Elm Street* (1984) has often been cited as one of Peele's favorite horror films. While there are several nods to the Wes Craven classic throughout *Us*, its influence is most notable in the makeup and costume design of the Tethered.

Interestingly, one of the VHS cassettes on the shelves isn't store bought. With the words "Thursday Nites" sprawled across a label in handwritten black ink, the suggestion is that the tape contains recordings from television. There are a host of options: In 1986, ABC aired *Ripley's Believe It or Not!*, which highlighted real-life strange occurrences, as well as the science fiction mystery series *Shadow Chasers*. On CBS, you'd find *Simon & Simon*, a comedy-drama series about a pair of brothers who were opposite in every way, but worked together to investigate and solve crimes.

The highest-rated Thursday-night program that year was *The Cosby Show*. The six-time Emmy Award–winning program was widely beloved during its initial run and for the decades that followed. Let's consider, for a moment, that the sitcom was recorded on the cassette. By the time *Us* was in production, the show's reputation had largely been marred by Bill Cosby's 2018 conviction for aggravated sexual assault. Though that ruling was ultimately overturned after *Us* was released, the cassette would serve as a covert allusion to discordance between Cosby's public persona as America's Dad and his monstrous alleged private actions, similar to Peele's commentary on Corey Feldman and Corey Haim. As if anticipating the concept of duality that runs throughout *Us*, Andrea Constand, one of his alleged victims, said in 2018, "We may never know the full extent of [Cosby's] double life."

Following the weather report, the television screen goes blank. When an image returns, it is jarring. "What has twelve million eyes," an omniscient narrator asks, as the image of sixty-eight eyes fills the screen, "a hundred and ninety-two million teeth," as sixteen sets of open-mouthed smiles now appear (before that number multiplies after a jump cut), "and stretches from the Golden Gate Bridge all the way to the Twin Towers?"

The answer is Hands Across America, the nationwide public demonstration ostensibly to raise money and build awareness to help people living in poverty. While the highly publicized pop-culture moment occurred in 1986, the effort has its origins in an identically named yet unrelated project that took place in 1975.

"The "Thursday Nites" cassette in particular references the HBO program *Thursday Night Prime* from the '90s, which ran B action or genre films with Cynthia Rothrock or Jeff Fahey that I remember watching obsessively."

—JORDAN PEELE

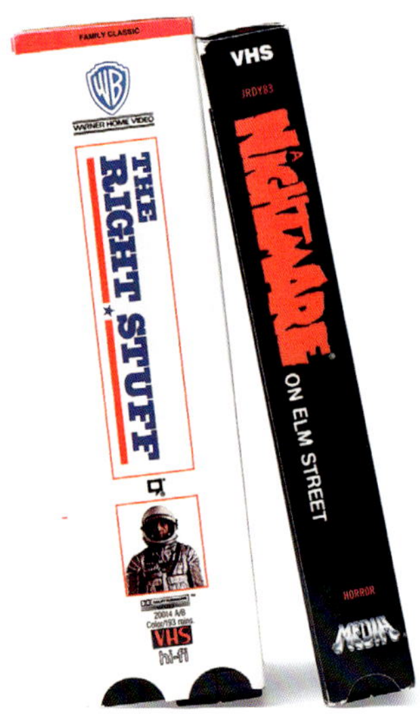

On a cloudy day in November of that year, nearly two thousand people lined a mile-long stretch of highway in Spring Arbor, Michigan, holding hands for five minutes while singing "God Bless America." For those few moments, the clouds parted and the sun came out. The demonstration was brief, but Marvin J. Rosenblum, who came up with the idea, said he hoped to replicate Hands Across America on Independence Day of the following year, in honor of the country's bicentennial.

"The feeling that our nation is divisive is a myth. This proves it," he said. "If this happens on a national basis, it will be an act of God. It's a needed psychological uplift to pull us out of the doldrums of Vietnam and Watergate.

"I was trying to imagine a line not from Dearing Road to Chapel Road, but from Los Angeles to Boston," he continued. "As emotional and electric as this was, that feeling would be multiplied many times with five million persons holding hands."

Rosenblum tried to interest the federal government to back the event as part of its bicentennial celebrations, but officials declined to get involved, citing the logistical challenges of getting people across the country to hold hands at the same time. Several celebrities, including Florence Henderson, the Osmonds, Paul Lynde, and Tony Orlando, signed on as honorary Hands Across America board members, but with Rosenblum unable to raise the requisite $25,000 he needed to get his idea off the ground, the idea fizzled out.

Hands Across America resurfaced in October 1985. Ken Kragen, a cofounder of USA for Africa, the nonprofit organization behind the all-star charity single "We Are the World" (which raised $44.5 million in one year to combat famine in Africa) announced the effort as an American-focused follow-up. The goal was for ten million people to form a "4,000-mile chain of humanity," with the hopes of raising up to $100 million through small-dollar donations from participants to address hunger in the United States.

Kragen's Hands Across America, which took place in May 1986, was immediately criticized in the press by activists as "a superficial gesture that offered no long-term solution to poverty in the United States." That assessment proved to be prophetic, as the demonstration fell far short of its fundraising goals. After paying off its expenses, the effort raised only about $15 million for charity, with most of that money going to long-term humanitarian efforts instead of providing immediate aid for those in need.

"The elaborate stunt aimed to raise money to help the poor . . . may have been the most eighties thing to happen in the '80s," Amy Argetsinger wrote in a 2016 *Washington Post* article. "It had all the save-the-world ambitions of the 'USA for Africa' campaign and an era-defining celebrity cast . . ., all wrapped in a kind of heart-on-sleeve patriotism that had seized the culture since the triumphs of the Soviet-free 1984 Olympics."

While writing *Us*, Peele stumbled on a commercial for a Hands Across America commercial that had aired on MTV in 1985, and he was struck by its eeriness. "There's something cultlike about the imagery that makes me think of the Manson family singing folk songs as they leave the courtroom," he says. "There's like an insistence that as long as we have each other, we can walk blindly past the ugliness and evil that we may be a part of."

"I don't think the notion is an evil one," he added, referring to Kagan's efforts, before stating that he felt the event was "more for the people who are holding hands to cure hunger than for the people who are hungry themselves."

In *Us*, the allusion to Hands Across America serves multiple purposes: On one level, it serves as a reminder that well-intentioned social movements can still end up being largely symbolic in nature. In the context of the film, Hands Across America is another source of inspiration for a young Adelaide, as she will eventually become an integral part of a large-scale social movement. The logo, as it appears within the universe of the film, is a line of interconnected red stick figures, representing "a chain of Good Samaritans" who "will tether themselves together"—language exclusive to the cinematic version of the commercial.

The significance of the word *tether* is clear, but what of the "Good Samaritan"? While it has become commonplace to use the term to refer to someone who generally does good things, the biblical parable that engendered it states that someone who earns that honorific must love their neighbor as they love themselves, for that is the only way to inherit eternal life. Once again, it's about interconnectedness.

Once the television commercial concludes, a reflection of a young Adelaide—Addy—can be seen on the television set. She appears frozen, transfixed as if she had been studying the images on the screen. She is holding a stuffed white rabbit, and as the camera continues to push in, upbeat music plays on the TV.

It is another commercial—bright and fun—this time for the Santa Cruz Beach Boardwalk, and within moments, we are actually there on the boardwalk with Young Addy, but we are no longer safe. We are no longer in front of the television set.

We are inside the nightmare.

PREVIOUS SPREAD: Red in the Underpass classroom with a Hands Across America paper chain.
OPPOSITE: The Wilsons' VHS cassette collection, which Young Addy draws inspiration from.
ABOVE: Young Addy's stuffed rabbit with its head untethered from its body.

MICHAEL JACKSON'S
THRILLER

CHAPTER 2

WHAC-A-MOLE

Peele has established that Addy is a careful observer, and as we jump to the Santa Cruz boardwalk, she continues to take everything in. It is her birthday, and her father is attempting to win her a prize by tossing a baseball at milk bottles while her mother looks on. We can't see their faces, but their body language speaks volumes. Russel, Addy's father, vacillates between having confident swagger and hopping up and down to burn off nervous energy. Rayne, her mom, seems emotionally detached, maintaining a comfortable distance. Addy takes it all in.

At his daughter's request, Russel wins her a black T-shirt with an image of a zombified Michael Jackson, flanked by two undead dancers on each side, in front of a logo in red capital letters: **MICHAEL JACKSON'S THRILLER**. Although Rayne opposes the shirt, remembering that the music video had given Addy nightmares, her impressionable daughter is nonetheless drawn to the already-iconic image.

OPPOSITE: Young Addy's Boardwalk prize—a Michael Jackson's Thriller t-shirt.
ABOVE: Young Addy with her parents on the Santa Cruz Boardwalk, 1986.

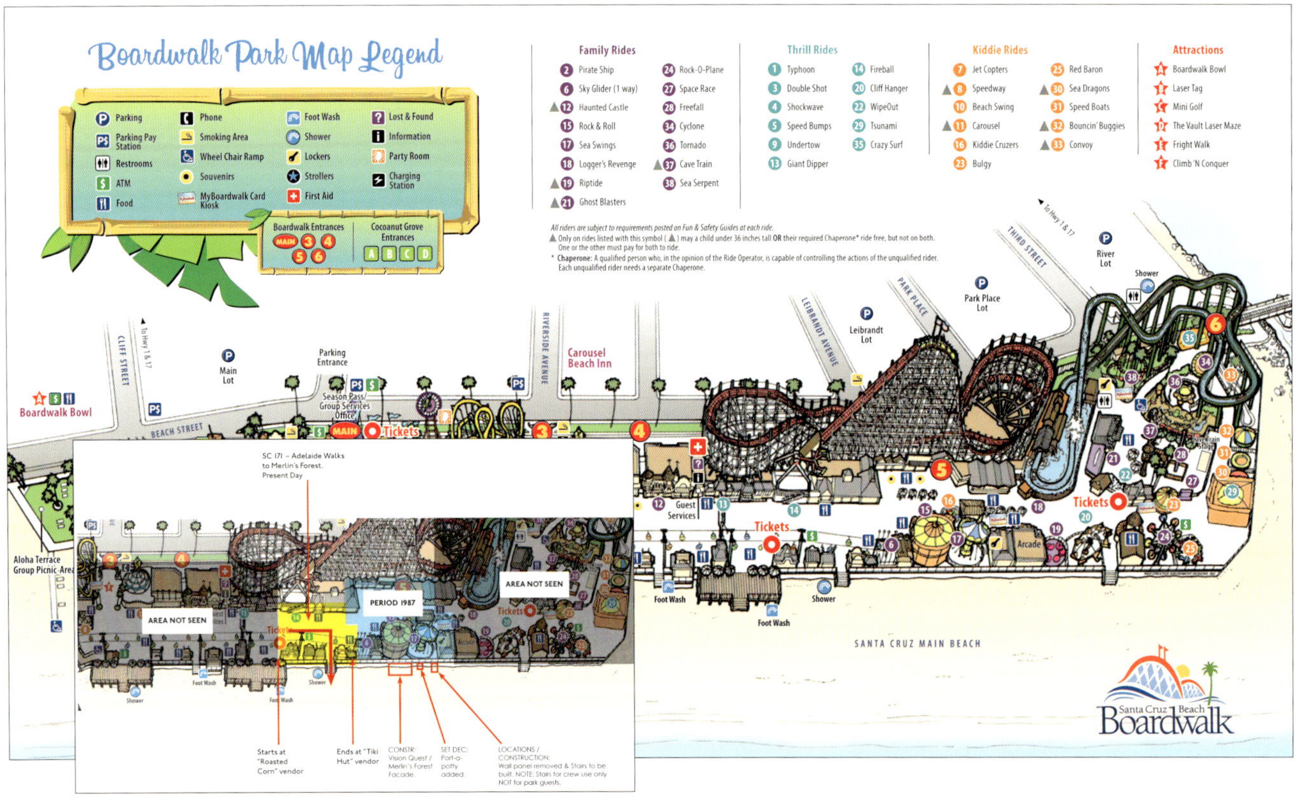

TOP: Addy watches as her father plays Whac-A-Mole.
ABOVE: A legend of the Santa Cruz Boardwalk, with filming locations notated by the production team.

Even before the music video was released on December 2, 1983, Michael Jackson's *Thriller* album was an instant chart topper and bestseller, buoyed not only by his critically acclaimed hit singles like "Billie Jean" and "Beat It" but also by the music video for the former song, the first by a Black artist to be played in heavy rotation on MTV, enshrining the album in the pantheon of popular culture.

In the United States, "Thriller" was the album's seventh and final single, and its accompanying music video was Jackson's magnum opus. The preliminary concept for the video originated from Jackson himself. "He loved a film I made called *An American Werewolf in London*," John Landis, who directed the music video, says. "And he was particularly taken with [makeup artist] Rick Baker's Oscar-winning work on the metamorphosis. He was fascinated, obviously, by transformation, and he wanted to turn into a monster."

The music video is both an homage to horror films and, in a way, a short horror film itself. Early on, we see Jackson transform into a werecat while on a date with his girlfriend, played by actress Ola Ray, before it's revealed that what we had just witnessed was part of a B-horror movie that the couple are watching in a crowded movie theater. The two leave the cinema, and as they pass by a graveyard, zombies start to rise from the underground. Jackson turns into one himself before leading a lengthy dance break of the undead.

"Thriller" changed the music video as a medium, and overnight, Jackson demonstrated the impact Black artists can have within the horror genre.

There is no doubt that by 1986, "Thriller" would be on Addy's radar. For Peele, the visual reference to the music video was about establishing *Us* in a specific era of time while encouraging the viewer to consider the legacy of Jackson, who faced controversy throughout his lifetime and posthumously.

"We've always known that there's a great duality to this man," Peele says. "This is a film about duality. 'Thriller' scared the pants off of me as a kid, and you have this figure who, on one hand, he's the most charismatic and positive guy, but there's also this clear darkness he's expressing."

Addy puts on the oversized shirt before walking with her parents to another beach boardwalk attraction, Whac-A-Mole. The carnival game, created in 1975, is simple in its gameplay: Using a soft mallet, the player beats down "moles"—underground creatures or individuals— that pop up from below. Unless one is incredibly coordinated, it's nearly impossible to keep them from breaking the surface. The sign above the game indicates that it takes 250 points to win a prize, but by the time the camera cuts away from Russel, who's bluntly beating down the game's intruders, he is far from achieving the requisite number. It appears the moles will win, but since Peele's camera follows Addy as she walks away, we are left not knowing whether the moles will emerge victorious.

ABOVE: The Whac-A-Mole prop.

Addy walks past a man further down the boardwalk holding a cardboard sign reading "Jeremiah 11:11." In numerology, 1111 is considered an "angel number," which some believe represents a new beginning. Visually, the number is another example of duality—two parallel pairs of ones.

The verse itself leaves room for interpretation. In the King James Bible, Jeremiah 11:11 reads, "Therefore thus saith the LORD, Behold, I will bring evil upon them, which they shall not be able to escape; and though they shall cry unto me, I will not hearken until them."

Simply put, God is not coming to the rescue—and perhaps even more chillingly, he is assuming responsibility for the impending evil that is to come.

While it's clear that the verse is about retribution, it's uncertain who—in the context of *Us*—will be the subject of the Lord's vengeance. Could it be those aboveground, who will find themselves under attack by the Tethered, or is it the Tethered themselves who are having evil put on them and, absent divine intervention, must take matters—and a pair of golden scissors—into their own gloved hands?

The answer, perhaps, is present elsewhere in frame. Addy passes a couple (one of whom, notably, is wearing a single glove) playing the hand game rock–paper–scissors. Each player shapes one of their hands in the form of one of those three items, and whoever selects the superior object—scissors beat paper, paper beats rock, rock beats scissors—is the winner. The couple, however, is deadlocked: *scissors, scissors, scissors*. They remain stuck in an endless cycle, with both parties believing that scissors will ultimately lead them to victory.

Addy approaches the steps to the beach. High above her, people are enjoying themselves on a rotating swing ride, but instead of turning her attention upward, Addy descends the stairs into the darkness. Once she reaches the bottom landing and walks out of frame, the camera turns skyward, fixed on the swing ride.

Above, it is well lit. There is fun. There is community. There is safety.

We are headed in the opposite direction.

As Addy walks toward the beach, the scene mirrors an experience eleven-year-old Jordan Peele had in the summer of 1989, when he was on vacation with his mother in Ocean City, Maryland. While standing on the boardwalk, he noticed a flurry of lightning piercing the night sky, headed toward the Atlantic Ocean. It was an incongruous sight, since it wasn't raining, but something about that moment stuck with him. "I felt alive," he says. "Special, as though I was being invited into some ancient pattern."

PREVIOUS SPREAD: Addy gazes at the Shaman's Vision Quest from the beach.
TOP: A Boardwalk patron holds a "Jeremiah 11:11" sign, which serves as both a warning and symbol of duality.
ABOVE: A closer look at the worn sign.

As the thunder claps and the lightning dances through the clouds, Addy sees her own ancient symbol—the facade for a boardwalk attraction called the Shaman's Vision Quest. There are colorful lights around the building perimeter, as well as around the darkened entryway. It is simultaneously foreboding and inviting. A large painted illustration of a Native American chief in a large feathered headdress is above the attraction's name. An otherwise disembodied hand is pointed in Addy's direction, confirming that the message written in lights above the door—"Find Yourself"—is, in fact, for her.

Peele has cited Stanley Kubrick's 1980 film *The Shining* as a source of inspiration for *Us*, and the Native American iconography in this scene hints at the movie's impact. Not only is the Overlook Hotel, *The Shining*'s primary location of terror, furnished with designs found among American Indigenous tribes, but also the hotel is described in the film as having supposedly been built on top of "an Indian burial ground."

On a base level, just like the man holding the biblical sign on the boardwalk, the shaman appears as an unexpected, and perhaps unwelcome, spiritual guide. However, something else seems to be at work: As *Us* is an allegory for American injustice and inequality, it is worth pondering what it means to have people search for themselves in the country's indigenous roots.

Like Addy, we are outside, uncertain as to what lies within and beneath. Our young human guide walks toward the facsimile of a spiritual guide, toward the arrow pointing downward, toward the Shaman's Vision Quest entrance.

She drops her blood-red candy apple into the sand. It is a wasteful act—a reminder that what some take for granted, others would cherish. As she prepares to step into the unknown, she leaves the forbidden fruit behind: "God has said, 'Ye shall not eat of it, neither shall ye touch it, or you will die.'"

Addy enters through the doorway as rain falls behind her. She has found cover. If the shaman keeps his promise, she will also find herself.

TOP: Young Addy's candy apple.
ABOVE: A detailed rendering of the Shaman's Vision Quest façade.

SET SCHEMATICS

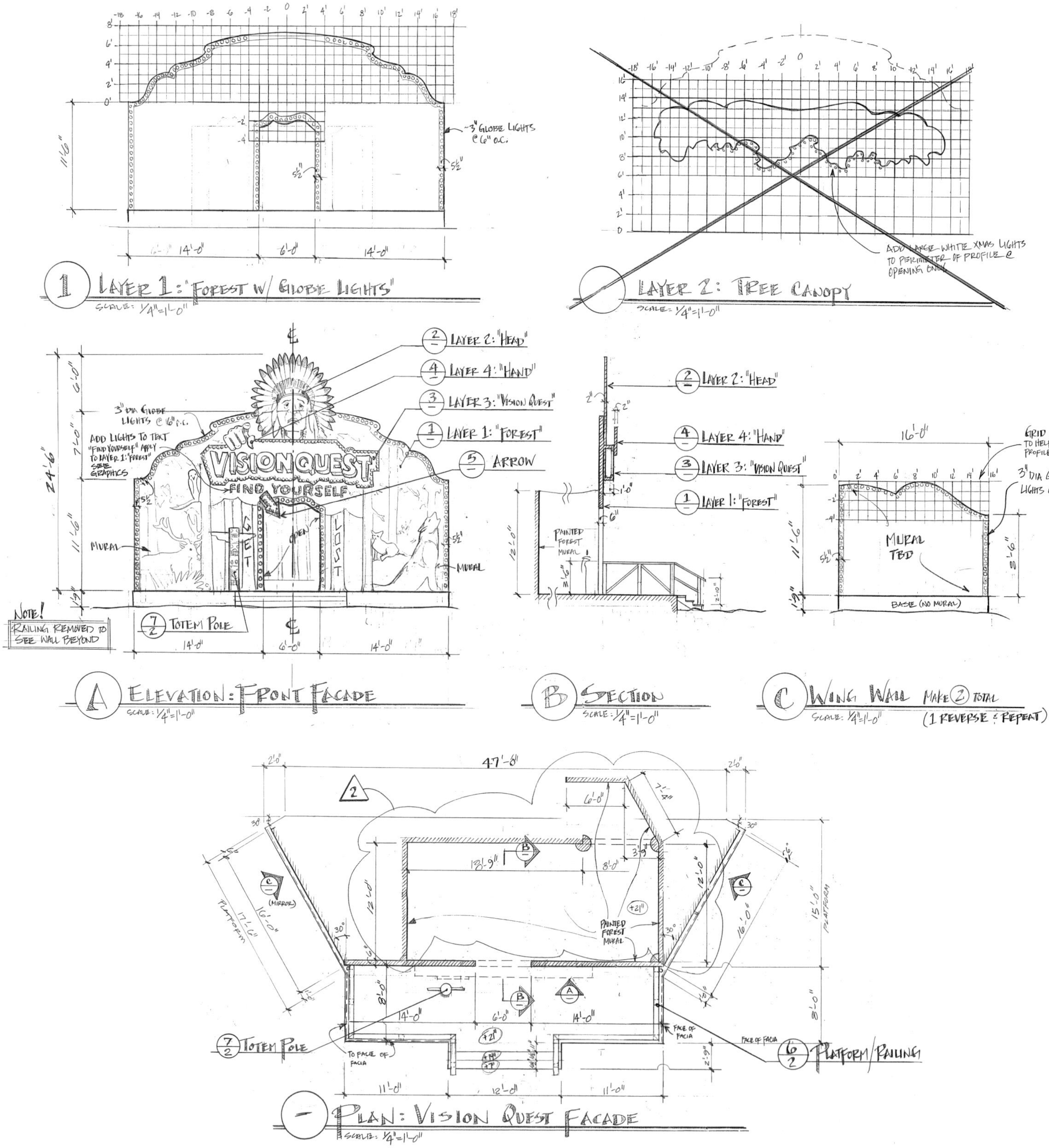

ABOVE AND OPPOSITE: The interior and exterior of the Shaman's Vision Quest.

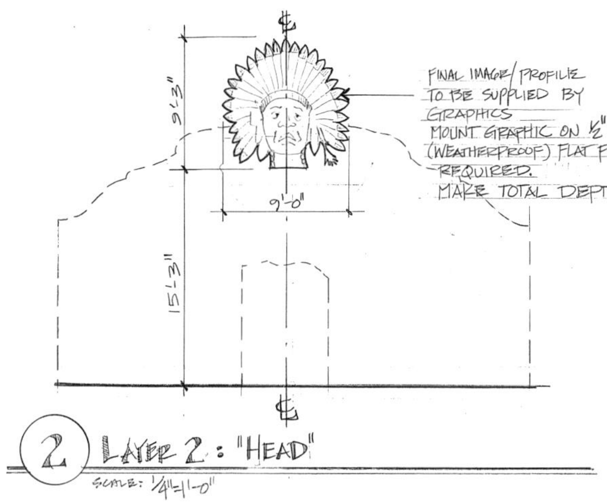
9'-3"
FINAL IMAGE/PROFILE TO BE SUPPLIED BY GRAPHICS
MOUNT GRAPHIC ON ½" SUBSTRATE (WEATHERPROOF) FLAT FRAME AS REQUIRED.
MAKE TOTAL DEPTH 2"
9'-0"
15'-3"
2 LAYER 2 : "HEAD"
SCALE: ¼"=1'-0"

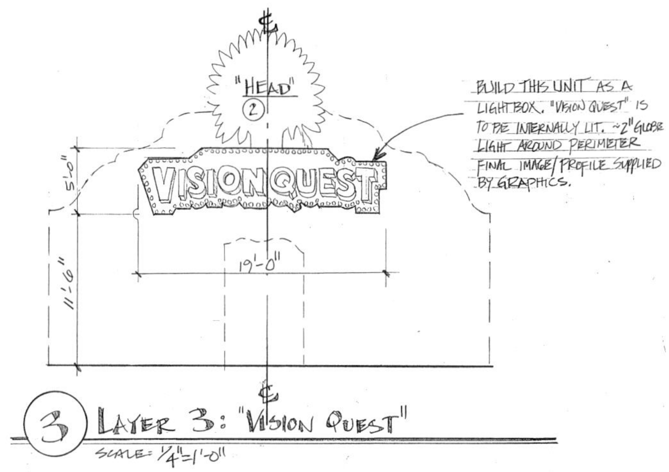
"HEAD"
2
BUILD THIS UNIT AS A LIGHTBOX. "VISION QUEST" IS TO BE INTERNALLY LIT. ~2" GLOBE LIGHT AROUND PERIMETER
FINAL IMAGE/PROFILE SUPPLIED BY GRAPHICS.
5'-0"
VISION QUEST
19'-0"
11'-6"
3 LAYER 3: "VISION QUEST"
SCALE: ¼"=1'-0"

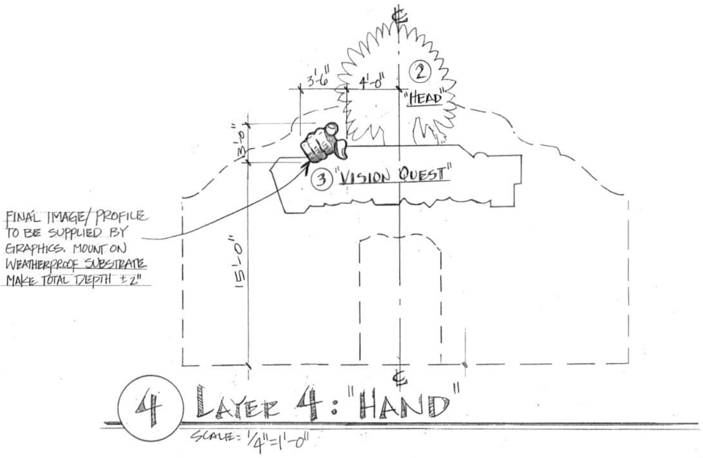
3'-6"
4'-0"
2
"HEAD"
3'-0"
3 "VISION QUEST"
FINAL IMAGE/PROFILE TO BE SUPPLIED BY GRAPHICS. MOUNT ON WEATHERPROOF SUBSTRATE MAKE TOTAL DEPTH ±2"
15'-0"
4 LAYER 4: "HAND"
SCALE: ¼"=1'-0"

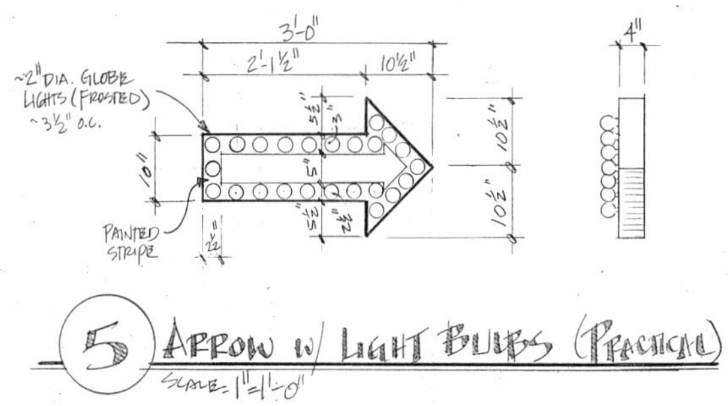
3'-0"
2'-1½"
10½"
4"
~2" DIA. GLOBE LIGHTS (FROSTED) ~3½" O.C.
10"
10½"
10½"
PAINTED STRIPE
5 ARROW W/ LIGHT BULBS (PRACTICAL)
SCALE: 1"=1'-0"

NOTE!
VISION QUEST FACADE SIGN TO CHANGE OVER TO MERLIN FACADE FOR SECOND HALF OF SHOOTING
1
ENCHANTED
Vision quest
FIND YOURSELF

ABOVE AND OPPOSITE: Reference photos of the Santa Cruz Boardwalk after the set build.

BOARDWALK PRIZE CENTER
CANDY
TOYS
ICE CREAM
BEACH SHACK
HOT DOG ON A STICK

PIZZA SLICE
ICE COLD SODA
HOT Buttered POPCORN
RAINBOW COTTON CANDY
ICE COLD POPSICLES
SOFT SERVE ICE CREAM
PRETZELS
ICE CREAM

MILK BOTTLE PYRAMID

CHAPTER 3

FIND YOURSELF

The inside of the Shaman's Vision Quest is designed to replicate an enchanted forest. There are tall redwood trees, most of them illustrated, but also some fabricated in three dimensions. The interior of the attraction is awash in a dark light, with a few sporadic yellow light bulbs close to the ceiling.

To create the look Peele desired for the Shaman's Vision Quest interior, production designer Ruth De Jong and art director Cara Brower drew inspiration from Clifton's Cafeteria, a popular restaurant in downtown Los Angeles that, until its closure in 2018, was known for its famous murals inspired by the redwood forests.

A recorded narration plays through a speaker system. The words are an excerpt of the Hopi creation story: "These, the earth and water, he divided into places from which life could spring," the narration says. "The mountains and the valleys and the waters were all where they belonged."

The narration refers to the work of Sotuknang, the Hopi creator god. In the creation story, he believes he has finished creating the world, until his uncle Taiowa, the sun spirit, reminds him that there is more work to do. "It is very good, but you are not done with it," he says. "Now you must create life of all kinds and set it in motion according to my plan."

OPPOSITE: The Shaman's Vision Quest mechanical owl prop.
ABOVE: Young Addy, moments away from finding herself inside.

TOP: The menacing mechanical owl as it asks, "Who? Who?"
ABOVE: Young Addy comes face to face with a nightmare in the Shaman's Vision Quest.

Taiowa's words are a reminder of a familiar adage: Sotuknang had focused on individual elements of the world, but Taiowa reminded him to also consider the forest, not just the trees. As Sotuknang says later in the story—the last words heard before the power goes out, leaving Addy in deeper darkness and silence—"Here now is endless space, but in the world, there is no joyful movement." The narration is a reminder of the importance of action. Those who remain static are failing to be truly alive.

As Addy is walking through the darkened forest, a mechanical owl emerges from a wall. Given that owls are often a symbol of wisdom and knowledge, its presence appears to be a warning that danger awaits, discouraging Addy from proceeding along her journey. It is worth noting that in Greek mythology, owls are also seen as protectors. In this darkened labyrinth, the owl—a nocturnal bird—can come alive and see what others cannot. It cannot go unnoticed that while Addy is on a search to "find herself," the prerecorded voice of the owl confronts her on her journey to ask a simple, yet important, question: "Who? Who?"

Immediately after Addy sees the owl, we discover alongside our heroine that the Shaman's Vision Quest is actually a house of mirrors.

Filming this sequence was a technical feat. Production designer Ruth De Jong and Cara Brower were tasked with designing a set capable of accommodating the actors, the cameras, and the film crew—and, most importantly, minimizing the chance that the camera would catch a crew member in frame.

The interior set was constructed and filmed at Universal Studios. "We researched many of these from various fairs and carnivals and came up with our own for both the period and contemporary versions," De Jong says, alluding to both the Shaman's Vision Quest

ABOVE LEFT: The interior set for the Shaman's Vision Quest is cleaned between takes.
ABOVE RIGHT: The totem pole built for the Shaman's Vision Quest exterior.

iteration of the house of mirrors and its Merlin's Forest counterpart, which appears later in the film. "That was a lot of fun, working with two-way mirrors that allowed the DP [director of photography] to shoot it without being seen."

"We wanted a very specific path that young Adelaide goes down into the hall of mirrors," Brower says. "So we did a lot of research on how actual halls of mirrors are built. We found some really good floor plans of how they're laid out and, luckily, it coincided with how Peele scripted it."

Once a floor plan was established, storyboard artist Eric Yamamoto worked with Peele to carefully plan out each shot. "I built a 3D model of the whole set, and that helped a lot," Yamamoto says. "Then I could have a rendering of what each of the mirrors would show."

"I loved that set," Brower says. "We couldn't really see how it was coming together until the day we were going to shoot, when it was fully enclosed with the mirrors, with the ceiling blacked out, with the lighting and the murals. It worked exactly how we wanted it to."

Within the narrative of the film, the hall of mirrors serves as the catalyst for Adelaide's lifelong trauma. As she walks by the reflective walls, her image distorts. We see two Adelaides in the same frame—and, just as we collectively begin gaining our bearings, the power outage occurs.

The sound of rain and Addy's heavy breathing replaces the recorded narration. She walks toward a glowing red exit sign, but she slams into a mirrored wall. As she looks around, the camera switches to her point of view. There is no shortage of exit signs, which hints at the paradoxical reality—for Addy, there may be no exit at all.

Lonely and afraid, she begins whistling "The Itsy-Bitsy Spider," the children's nursery rhyme, in an attempt to calm her nerves.

Lyrically, the song is a story of persistence. The rain—not unlike the storm beyond the Shaman's Vision Quest walls—keeps washing the spider down the spout, but because it is patient and committed to its goal, the spider waits for the perfect opportunity to rise from below and climb to the top. It rejects the natural order, knowing that eventually, the conditions will be right for the spider to get what it wants. Spiders are strategic, patient predators, meticulously creating webs and waiting for their prey. Addy, unknowingly, is approaching one of those set traps.

Addy continues whistling until she hears the tune being returned to her by an unseen entity. She looks around for the source of the sound, or maybe for the exit, and eventually finds herself face to face with her doppelgänger.

The Shaman's prophecy has come true. She has found herself.

OPPOSITE: Eric Yamamoto's storyboards for the Shaman's Vision Quest sequence where Young Addy meets her doppelgänger.

ADELAIDE *VERSUS* RED

VISION QUEST
Get Lost
BAD

SET SCHEMATICS

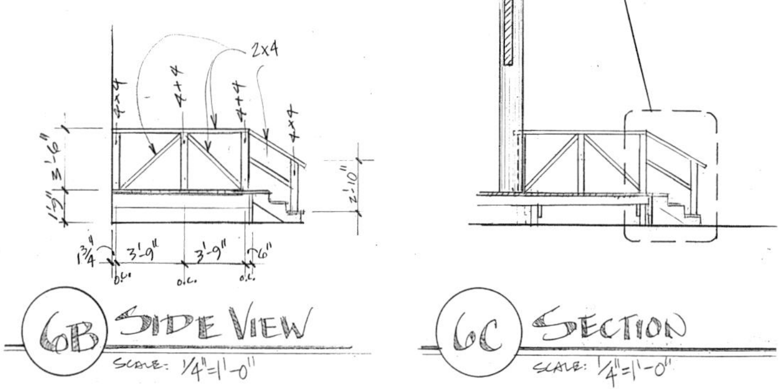

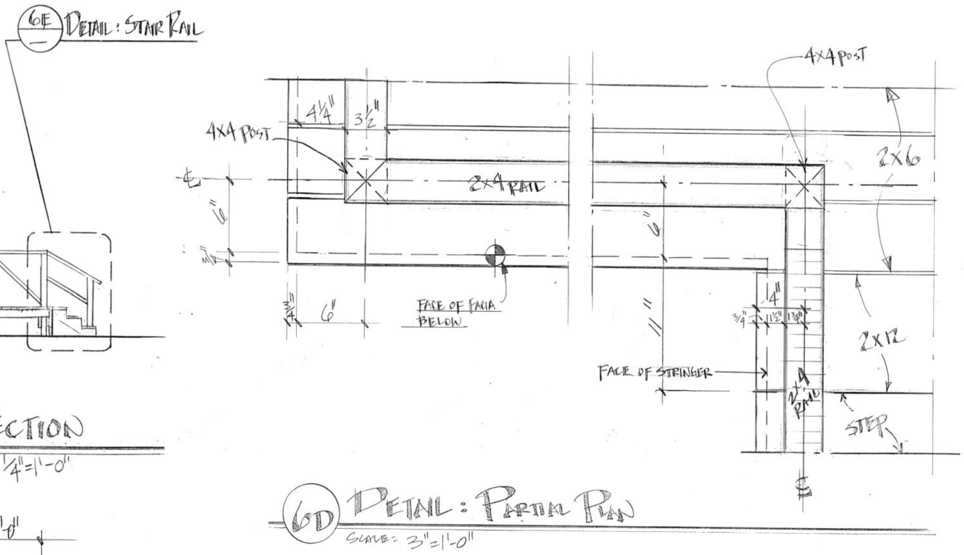

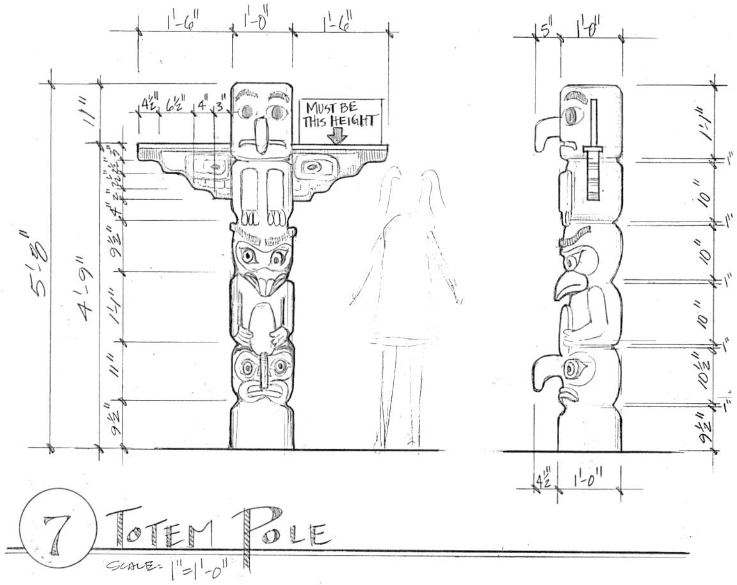

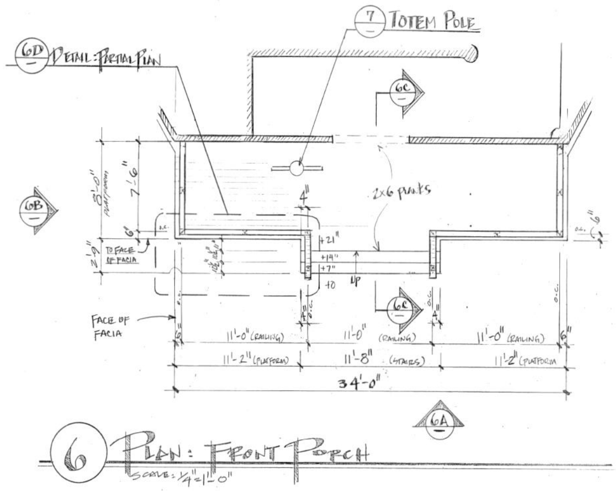

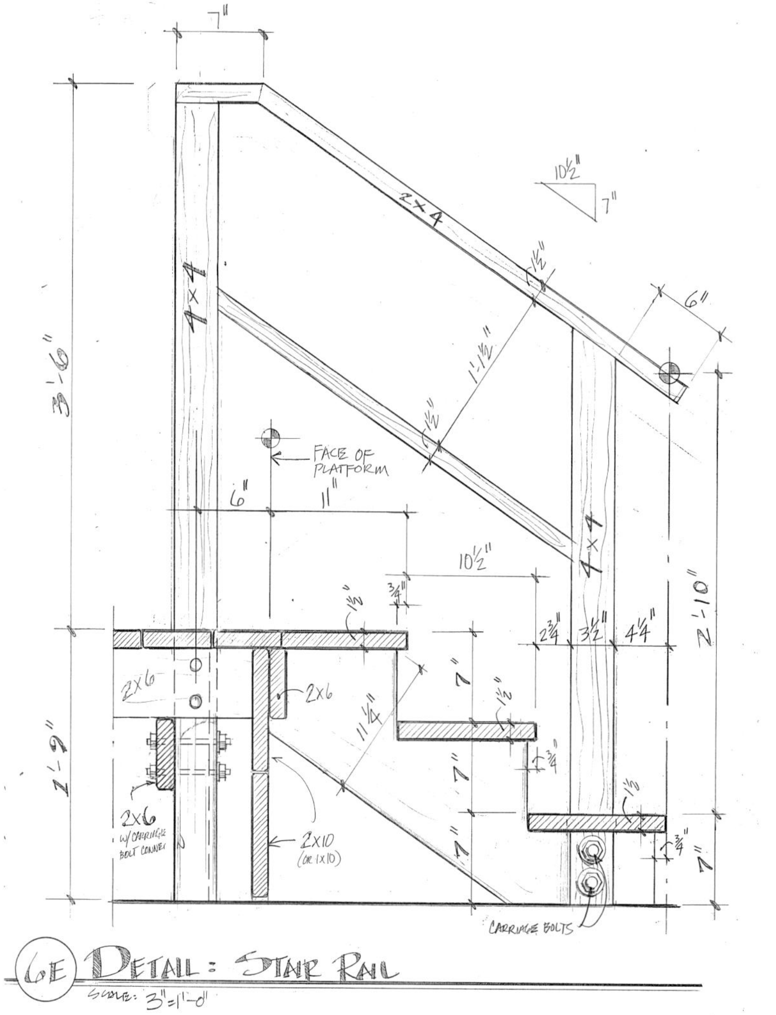

ABOVE AND OPPOSITE: The exterior of the Shaman's Vision Quest and the interior of the hall of mirrors set.

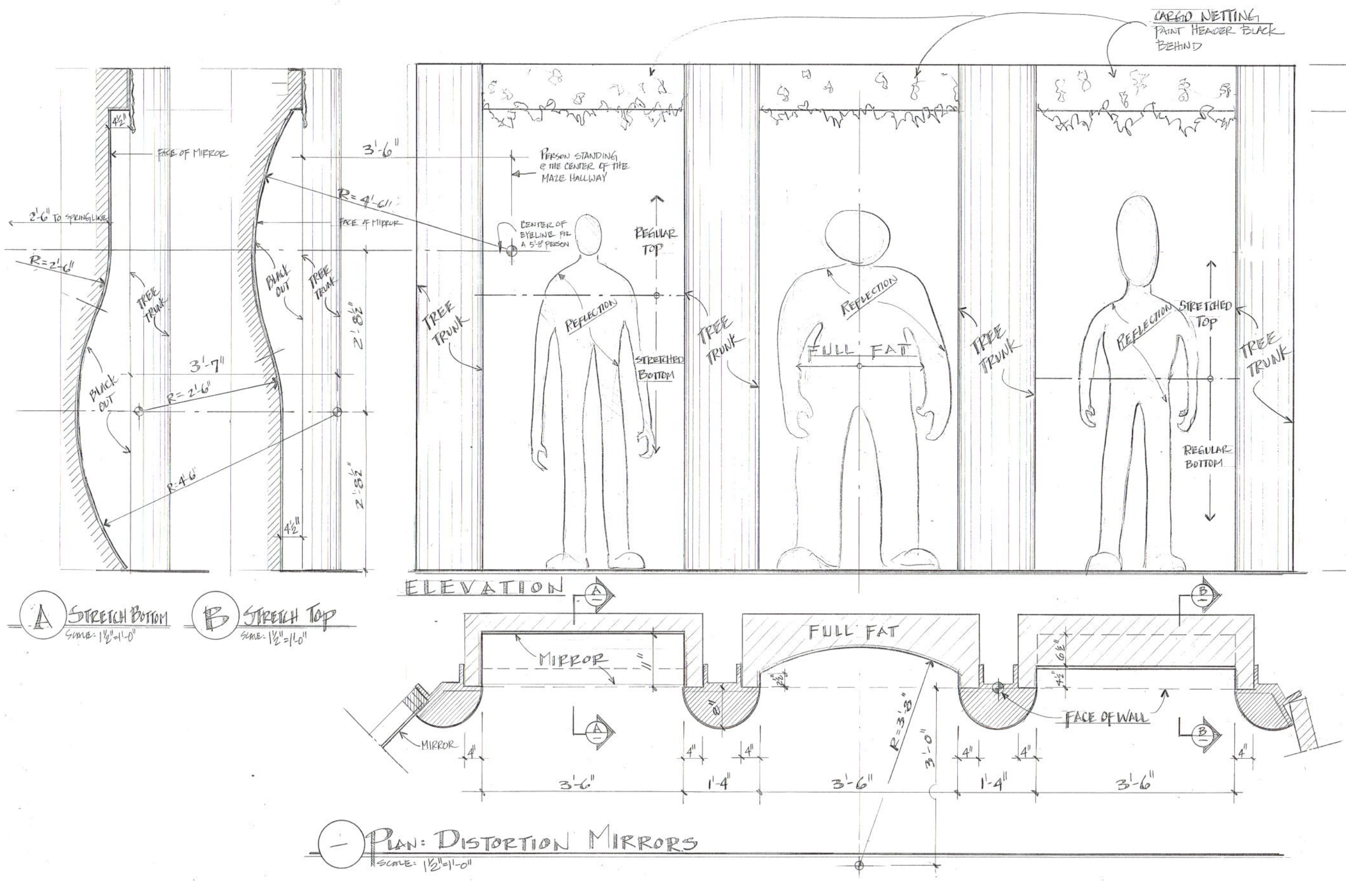
CARGO NETTING
PAINT HEADER BLACK BEHIND
FACE OF MIRROR
PERSON STANDING @ THE CENTER OF THE MAZE HALLWAY
CENTER OF EYELINE FOR A 5'0" PERSON
REGULAR TOP
STRETCHED BOTTOM
REFLECTION
FULL FAT
STRETCHED TOP
REGULAR BOTTOM
TREE TRUNK
BLACK OUT
ELEVATION
A STRETCH BOTTOM
B STRETCH TOP
MIRROR
FACE OF WALL
PLAN: DISTORTION MIRRORS

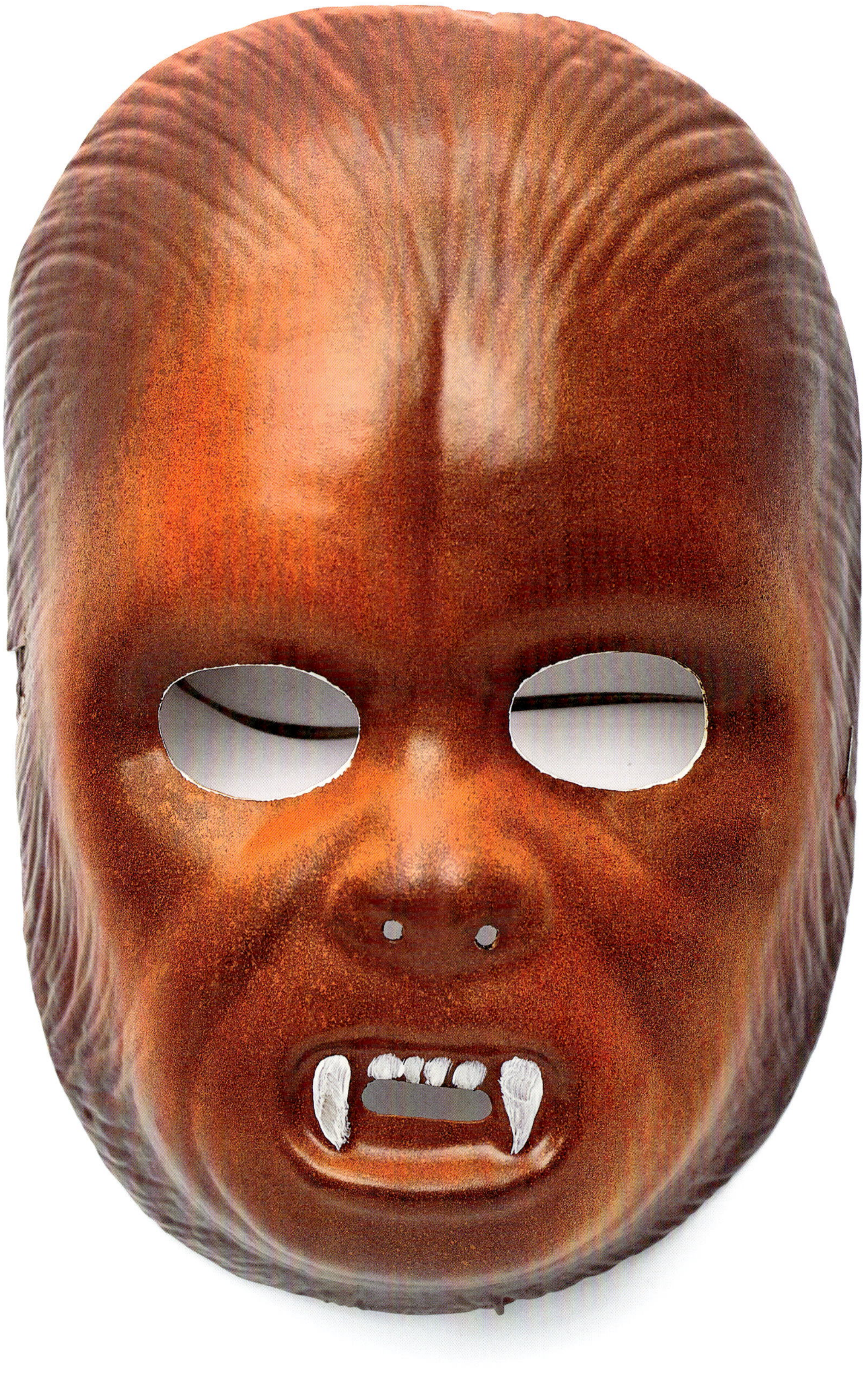

CHAPTER 4

THREE POINTING BACK AT YOU

After the title sequence, *Us* jumps to the present day. Before we have a chance to meet the Wilsons, the film's protagonists, we see a facsimile of them. There's a sticker on the back window of their car depicting a son, father, mother, and daughter holding hands—tethered, like the figures in the Hands Across America logo. The family is happy, and the seemingly simple sticker reinforces the film's themes of duality. In sticker form, the Wilsons can look outside into the world as well as within its interior. There are two parts, two dimensions. They have dual perspectives.

Additionally, each family member has at least two affinities and two counterparts. There are two males and two females, and among the children and adults, their complement is of the opposite gender. Their similarities equal their differences.

Within moments, we meet the Wilsons in human form. Adelaide, the young Addy who we have been following thus far, is now a mother. She is played by Academy Award winner Lupita Nyong'o, best known to audiences for her roles in *12 Years a Slave* and *Black Panther*. "Lupita is someone audiences feel they can access and have an identification with," producer Ian Cooper says. "She's someone you want to spend time with, but she's also so good at turning the screw a bit and making you feel suddenly alienated as well. That duality in her performance was perfect for this film, on multiple levels."

OPPOSITE: Jason's werewolf mask, which provides protection and strength.
ABOVE: The Wilson family, in sticker form, on their vehicle's back window.

"I had to prepare and develop a roadmap for myself," Nyong'o says. "With Adelaide . . . we spoke a lot about her pursuit of normalcy. She doesn't want anything but to pass. That's her thing. She has a deep, dark secret, and she's not trying to gain any attention."

Winston Duke, Nyong'o's *Black Panther* costar, is Adelaide's husband, Gabe. In many ways, the two are opposites. Adelaide is thoughtful, while Gabe is more impulsive. When it comes to parenting, Adelaide exhibits a quiet steadiness; Gabe is loud and more interested in having fun. "He's kind of a goofy dad, but he has an enthusiasm and spontaneity that makes him the spirit of the family," Peele says.

"I love Gabe's spectrum. He isn't just one thing. He's not an action hero. He's not just comedic. He's a full human being who has needs, desires, flaws, strengths," Duke says. "With this role, I knew I had the opportunity for drama, comedy, anxiety. All of that made him really attractive to me."

For the role of teenage daughter Zora, Peele cast Shahadi Wright Joseph, an actress previously seen in the Broadway adaptations of *The Lion King* and *School of Rock*. "Zora is a very relatable thirteen-year-old," Peele says. "She's a little snarky, she's smart and hitting a point in her life where she wants to be taken seriously as a young woman, but she's finding a bit of resistance from her parents as she tries to break out of that box."

Jason, the youngest member of the Wilson family, was played by Evan Alex in his feature film debut. From the first moments we meet him, it's clear that Jason is a bit different from the rest of his family. "He's an observer, and tends to get distracted," Alex says. "He's kind of in his own world. He's also really into magic tricks, while most boys his age are into sports. He has a magic ring that he's always playing with."

ABOVE LEFT: Winston Duke as Gabe Wilson, ready to confront the Tethered. **TOP RIGHT:** Peele, Jason, and Zora on set. **ABOVE RIGHT:** Jason's magic ring.

The ring is first seen when the Wilsons arrive at their family's vacation home, the residence once owned by Adelaide's late mother, Rayne. With its skull and its ability to produce fire, there's an incongruity with this piece of jewelry being on a child's hands. In this scene and throughout the film, Jason manipulates the ring's mechanism but is frequently unable to get it to light. In a sense, Jason is our Prometheus—intelligent, defiant, and drawn to the promise and potential of a flame. If he can get his ring to work at the right time, it may be the greatest gift he can give to humanity.

Jason is never seen without his werewolf Halloween mask, which he often wears on top of his head, pointed toward the ceiling. In many cultures around the world, mythological creatures are symbols of duality: They are one thing by day, another by night, and their transformation is often caused by a natural occurrence such as the sunset. Simultaneously, the werewolf is both a person and a creature imposing on a person.

The scene around the dining table is reminiscent of those in Steven Spielberg films like *E.T. the Extra-Terrestrial*, which also centers on an American family and otherworldly creatures. For Peele, *Us* was an opportunity to pay homage to the films he grew up loving as a kid while also reimagining how those films might have differed if a Black family was at the center of the story.

"There are elements of this film that follow in the Amblin tradition of a family working through their dynamic—*Poltergeist*, *Jaws*, *Close Encounters*," he says. "When I realized we haven't gotten a Black family in that scenario, I realized that there was a whole different reason this movie was important, even though the movie itself, plotwise, is not about race."

ABOVE: Jason armed with his werewolf mask and ring.

THIS PAGE: The Wilson's last supper.

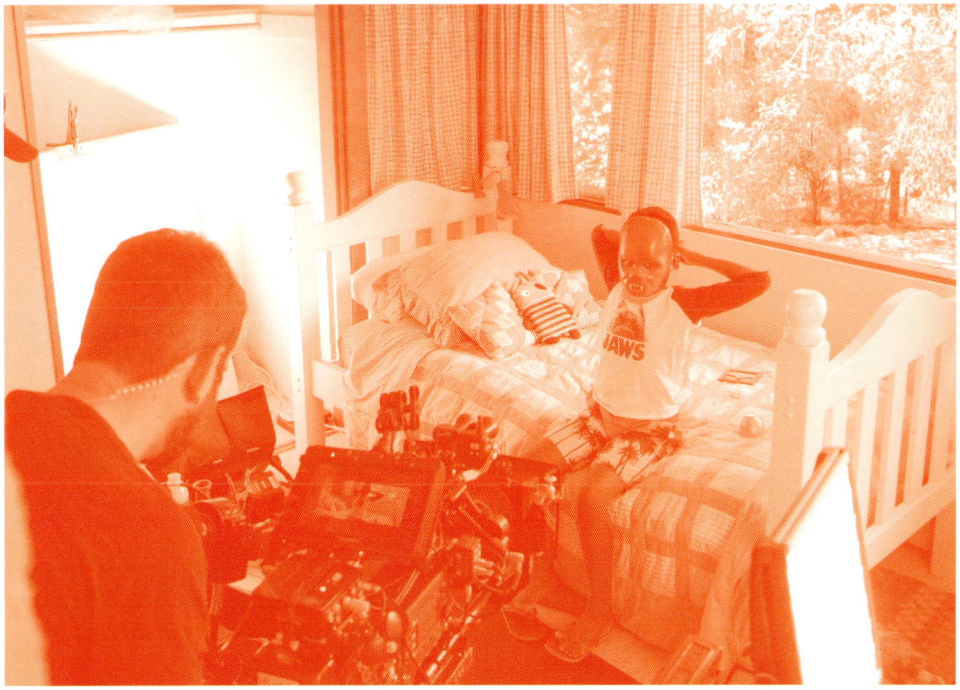

"In *Get Out*, the subject on the table was race and its paradigms and how that can affect and afflict one," Lupita Nyong'o says. "In *Us*, it's class and privilege, and the fact that we have a Black family taking us through the story is a matter of circumstance. It's not the exceptional thing, and that in itself I find radical and refreshing. People of color don't always see the world through the color of their skin."

Finding the perfect location for the Wilson's lake house was key to establishing the tone Peele wanted for *Us*. Production designer Ruth De Jong and her team searched for a location that could be used for both interior and exterior shots. Two hundred homes later, location manager Justin Duncan found a perfect place within Pasadena's North Kinneloa Ranch gated community.

When it came to dressing the Wilson home, De Jong, set decorator Florencia Martin, and art director Cara Brower carefully considered Adelaide's family history. While Rayne, Adelaide's mother, is seen only briefly in the opening scene and intermittently throughout the remainder of *Us* in flashback, every detail down to the photographs and furniture were deliberately chosen to advance our understanding of where Adelaide came from. Landscape paintings adorn the walls, as well as framed vintage posters for the Alvin Ailey American Dance Theater.

"The family had put young Adelaide in ballet classes, so we started from the idea that her family was very interested in the arts, and in design and architecture," Brower says. "We decided on a mid-century house, and then tried to bring that family history into it."

While at the table, the Wilsons enjoy what might be described as their last supper, a spread of fast food courtesy of Copperpot's Cove, a fictional restaurant chain created for the film. Interestingly, while the rest of her family partakes in the ultra-processed meal, Adelaide opts to partake in a bowl of bright red strawberries.

TOP: Photographs in the Wilson home, highlighting the importance of family history.
ABOVE: Filming Evan Alex in Jason's vacation home bedroom.

ABOVE: Production photos of the interior of the Wilson home.

SET SCHEMATICS

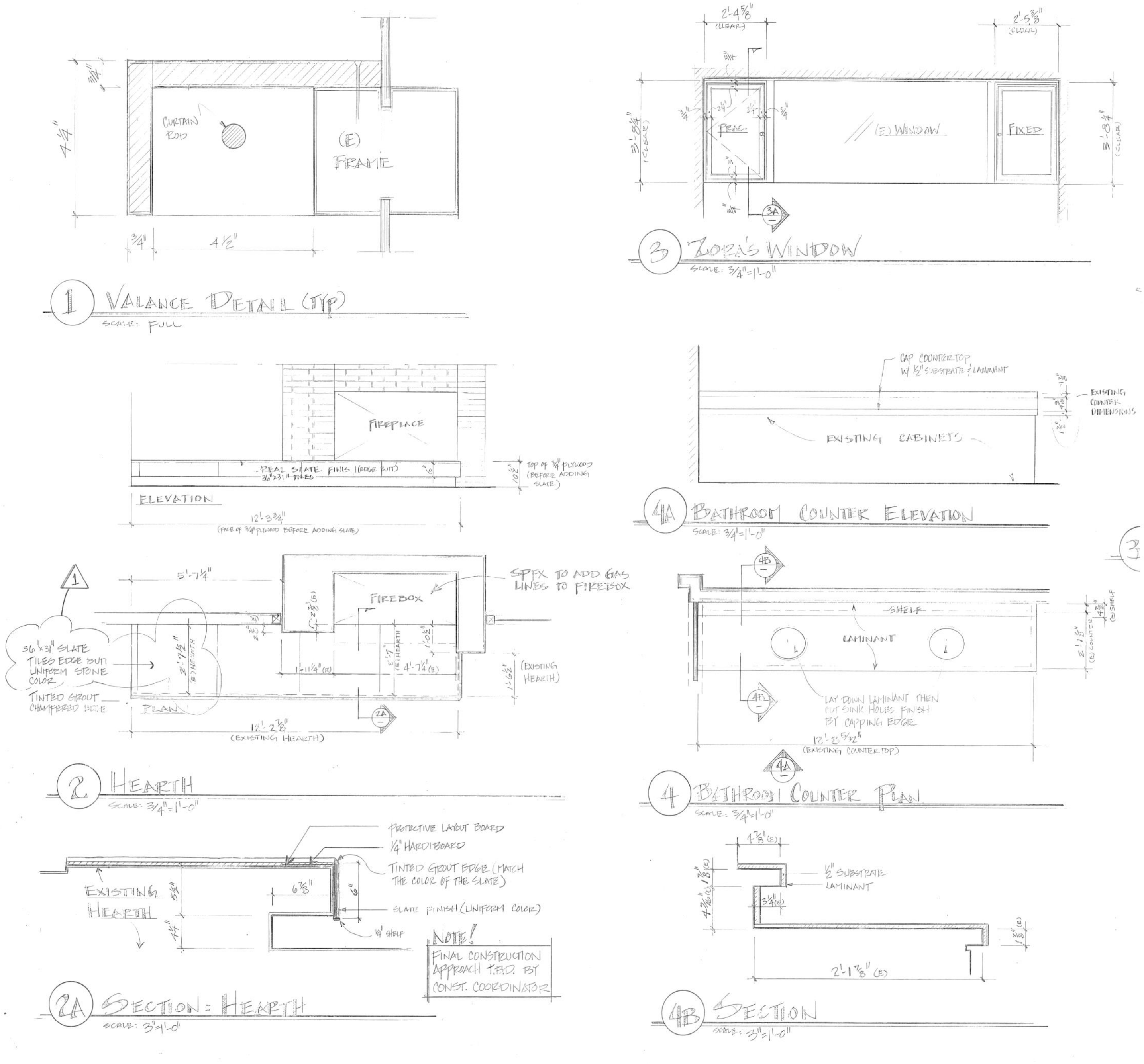

ABOVE: The augmentations made to the Wilson family home shooting location.

Literary scholars have noted that William Shakespeare's use of strawberries in both *Richard III* and *Othello* symbolize hypocrisy, deception, and a harbinger of death disguised behind a disarming and friendly facade. While her family settles into their vacation banter, Adelaide's mind drifts from their conversation toward a childhood memory of a visit to a psychiatrist. Mentally, she is somewhere else. One wonders where else distance exists between the matriarch and the rest of her family.

Later, Adelaide discovers a box of her childhood belongings in the basement. The first item she notices is a stuffed white bunny, a seemingly trivial plaything; however, for the viewing audience, it stirs up a memory. The film's title sequence began with the camera transfixed in a close-up on a live caged rabbit. After a few moments, cinematographer Michael Gioulakis slowly reveals that the isolated animal isn't alone—there is an entire wall of caged rabbits. The image is both startling and disorienting.

"That was a tricky shot," Gioulakis says. "Jordan had a temp version of the music cue from the composer Michael Abels, so we were able to time the shot out to the cue. We did a couple rehearsals and got it in maybe three or four takes. Because of the framing and some of the bunny performances, they ended up using the first take in the movie."

The stuffed animal seems to hold special meaning for Adelaide, just as rabbits will remain a significant part of *Us* throughout the duration of the film.

Adelaide's next memory is triggered by seeing a photograph of her younger self at dance class. Peele films the flashback sequence masterfully, encapsulating the theme of duality in multiple ways. As adult Adelaide holds the picture in her hand, she also sees a vision of young Addy next to a mirror at the ballet barre. The resulting shot puts four versions of the character in the same frame, with the focus on the young girl and her reflections, in some ways harkening back to the earlier Shaman's Vision Quest sequence.

We survey her in the past and the present.

As the young Addy turns towards the mirror, she appears to lock eyes with Adelaide. Once again, she has found herself.

ABOVE: Adelaide's box of childhood memories.

TOP: Young Addy looks up at her father.
ABOVE: Adelaide remembers dancing in her youth.

JAWS

SET SCHEMATICS

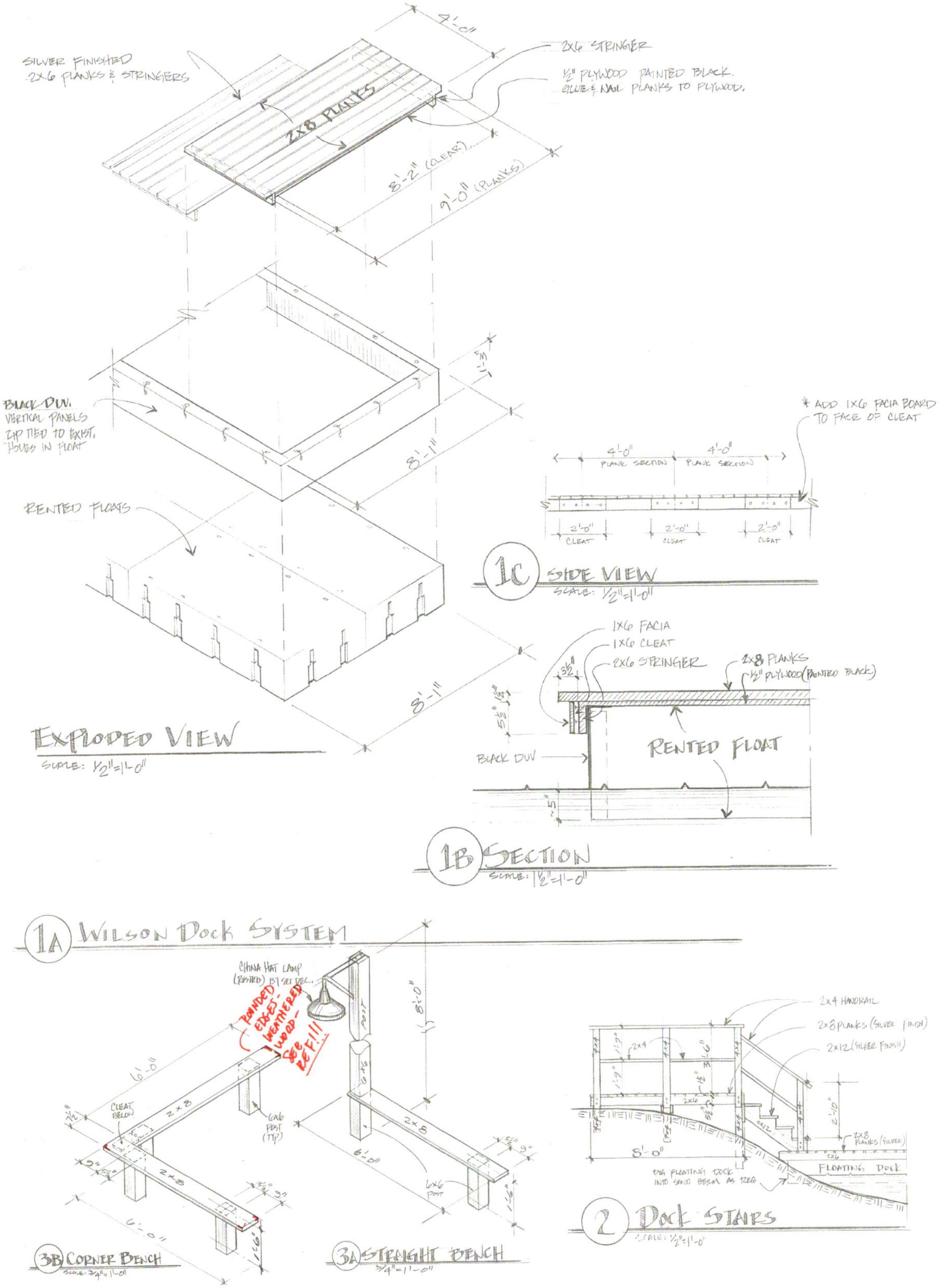

PREVIOUS SPREAD: Jason, Adelaide, and Zora at the dock.
ABOVE AND OPPOSITE: The dock outside the Wilson home.

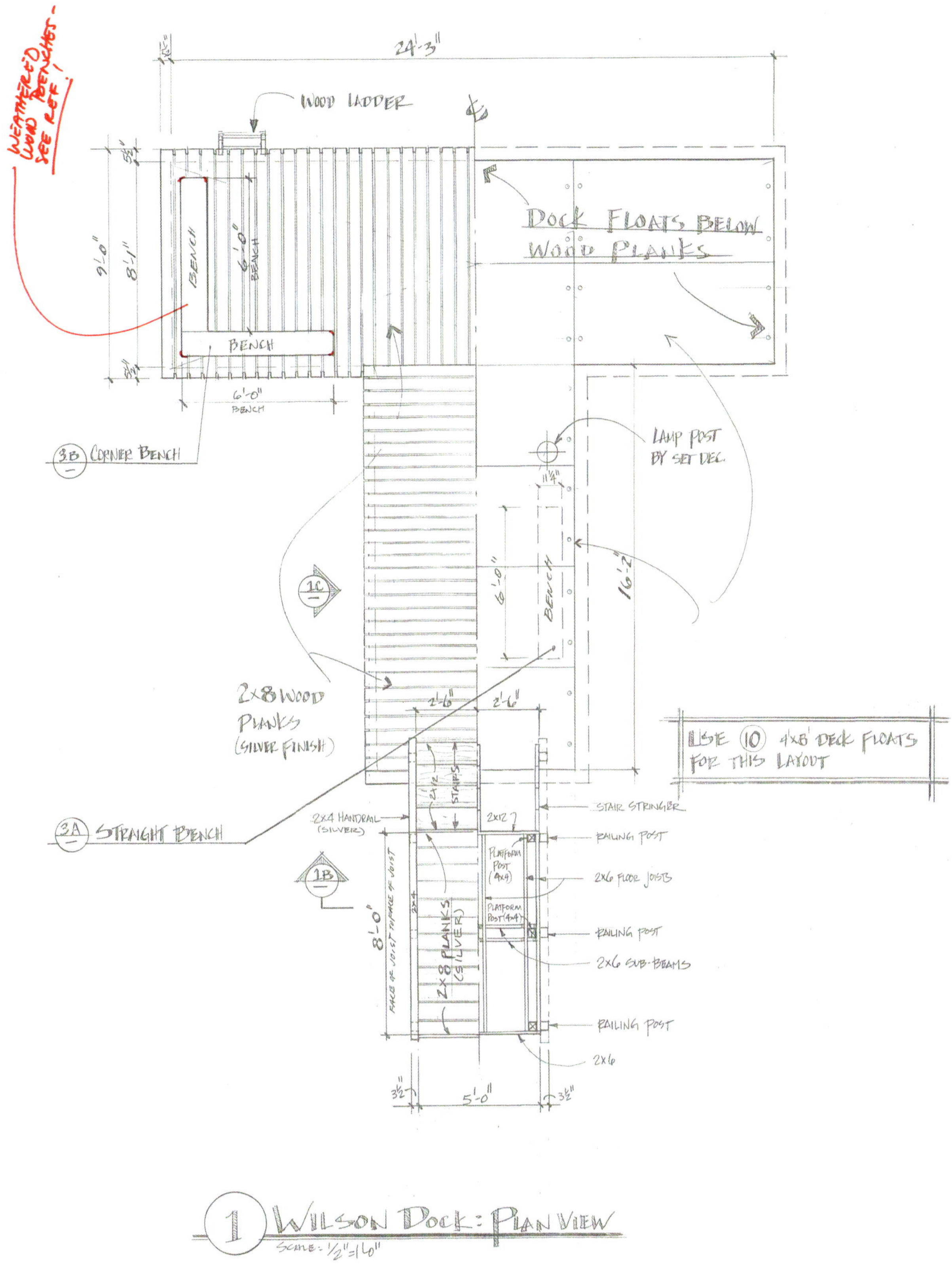

24'-3"
WOOD LADDER
DOCK FLOATS BELOW WOOD PLANKS
BENCH
6'-0" BENCH
BENCH
9'-0"
8'-1"
6'-0" BENCH
3B CORNER BENCH
LAMP POST BY SET DEC.
1C
6'-0"
BENCH
16'-2"
2x8 WOOD PLANKS (SILVER FINISH)
2'-6"
2'-6"
USE 10 4'x8' DECK FLOATS FOR THIS LAYOUT
3A STRAIGHT BENCH
2x4 HANDRAIL (SILVER)
STAIRS
2x12
STAIR STRINGER
RAILING POST
PLATFORM POST (4x4)
2x6 FLOOR JOISTS
1B
8'-0"
2x8 PLANKS (SILVER)
RAILING POST
2x6 SUB-BEAMS
RAILING POST
2x6
3½"
5'-0"
3½"
1 WILSON DOCK: PLAN VIEW
SCALE: ½"=1'-0"

CHAPTER 5

5 ON IT

On their drive to the Santa Cruz beach, Gabe turns on the radio and finds "I Got 5 on It," the 1995 single by California-based rap group Luniz. The song was a hit, selling over a million copies in the United States and topping the charts in the United Kingdom and the Netherlands. To the Wilsons, "I Got 5 on It" provides a welcome diversion as Jason has just used the word *anus*, which shocks, disgusts, and mildly amuses the rest of his family. For the audience, the song establishes a musical motif composer Michael Abels revisits at several key moments in the film.

"It was in the script," Abels says. "My memory is that the scene in the car was written knowing that the song was going to be in it."

After working with Peele on *Get Out*, Abels was invited to join the *Us* creative team early in the process. For the composer, this was a sign that the score would be just as important as the film's visual elements, a presumption that ultimately proved to be correct.

"In preproduction, filmmakers will design the visual look of the world of the story, but I think [Peele] very much likes to design the auditory world too, which includes sound and music," he says. "He sent me the script and he said, 'So, obviously it's about duality, so give me some instruments that don't go together.'"

PREVIOUS SPREAD: Peele and Jason on set with an alternate werewolf mask.
OPPOSITE: A not so itsy-bitsy toy spider. **ABOVE:** Adelaide and Gabe drive to Santa Cruz.

To supplement his original score, Abels welcomed the opportunity to include well-known popular music into the film, just as he had done to great effect on *Get Out*. "I love doing it," he says. "There's always a lot of possibility artistically, but budgets and stakeholders and lawyers sometimes make it so that using popular music is not possible."

Even before the film's release, "I Got 5 on It" helped create both excitement and fear among the viewing audience, due to it being prominently featured in the theatrical trailer. In addition to the familiar version of the song, the advertisement included a slowed-down, sinister-sounding version, which would later be known as "The Tethered Mix." The fan reaction to the spot led to Abels revisiting the film's conclusion, a balletic battle between Adelaide and her doppelgänger, which was originally set to Tchaikovsky's *The Nutcracker*. "It was actually going to be pretty scary, but the trailer was a cultural phenomenon, so that music idea was abandoned," Abels says. "Jordan knew. He said, 'It's got to be '5 on It,' and of course, it had to be."

"Some filmmakers are a little shy, or have some anxiety about screenings of a film," Abels continues. "All I've ever seen from Jordan is enthusiasm for test screenings. He's not afraid of leaning into an audience response and adapting the film to respond to it. When people responded to the trailer, I think he felt like, 'Well, we absolutely have to make sure that 'The Tethered Mix' is part of the film, and that the excitement that people had about the trailer is realized."

"I feel like the beat in that song has this inherent cryptic energy, almost reminiscent of the *Nightmare on Elm Street* soundtrack," Peele says.

The instrumental composition of "I Got 5 on It" follows a musical call-and-response. For Abels, this provided an entry point to amplify the film's narrative message. "When it's first played, the song is just a great way to understand the family, who they are as a unit, and how they relate to each other," Abels says.

"What's interesting about it—which I didn't realize until we started messing with it—is how it fits in with the duality theme," he continues. "In the sample of that song, which is Club Nouveau's 'Why You Treat Me So Bad,' the bass line is like a melody in itself, so it's really got two melodies, a low one and a high one. When it was time to score the dance fight, I had a call-and-response already set up."

Even though the original, unaltered version of the song plays in the car with the Wilsons, Peele and Abels still use "I Got 5 on It" to hint at future horror.

As the family approaches the beach, immediately adjacent to the boardwalk, with Gabe behind the driver's seat chanting, "Santa Cruz! Santa Cruz!" with his fist in the air, the song starts to recede into the background. Gabe's voice becomes distorted as Adelaide briefly revisits another childhood memory. The sound of an ambulance brings her mind back to the present. The Wilsons see a man, bloodied, being lifted into the back of the emergency vehicle. He is holding a familiar cardboard sign—Jeremiah 11:11.

As the family arrives at the site of Adelaide's childhood trauma, her past and present are becoming one.

ABOVE AND OPPOSITE: The reappearance of Jeremiah 11:11.
FOLLOWING SPREAD: A toy spider and its real-life counterpart at the Wilson's house.
PAGES 60–61: Peele gives Nyong'o direction at the Wilson's dock set.

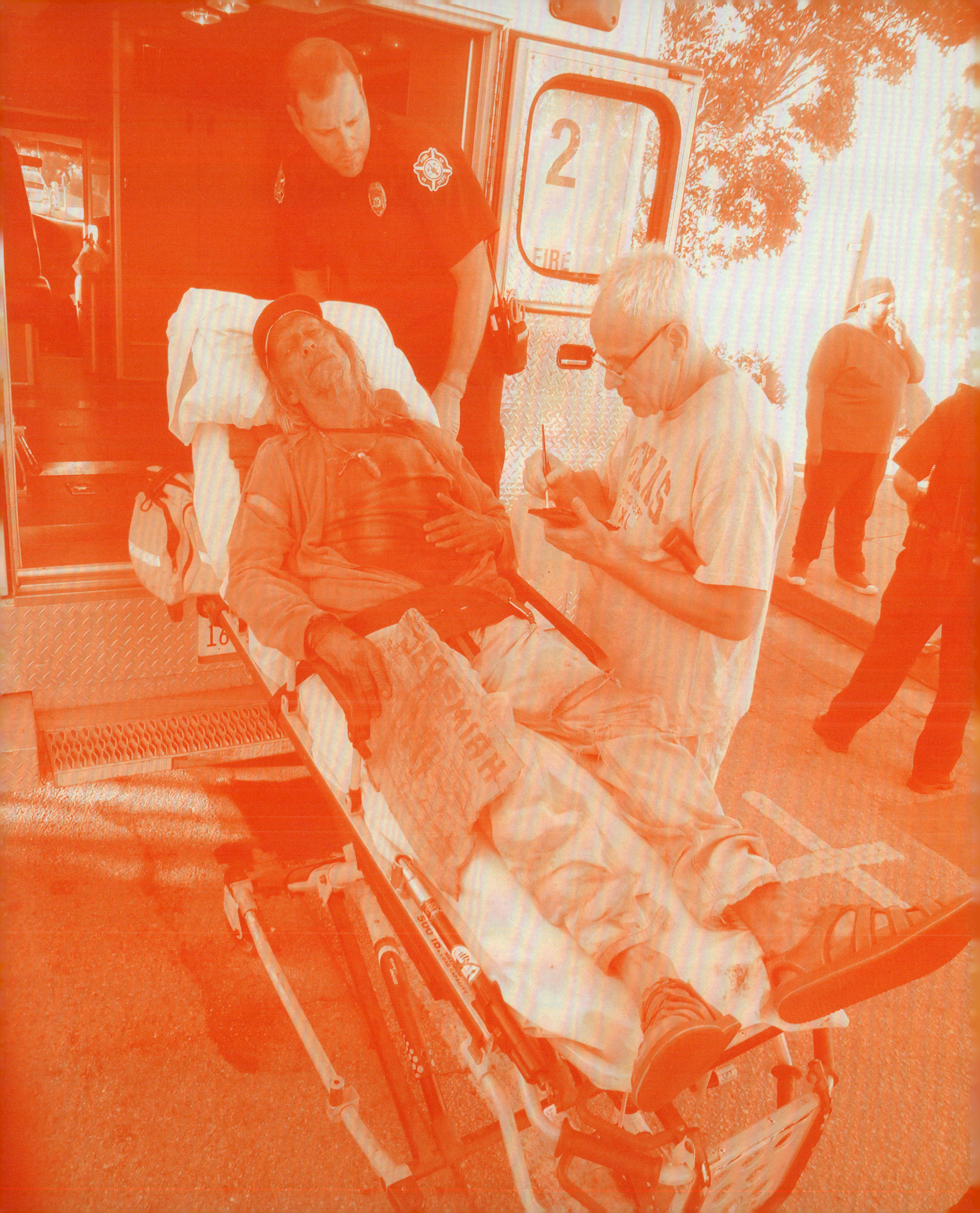
2
FIRE
TEXAS

"The song has always had a bit of character to it in that the bass line reminds me of Angelo Badalamenti's work on *A Nightmare on Elm Street* and *Twin Peaks: Fire Walk with Me*. I was intrigued with the notion of starting the film with a well-known hip-hop song that had a sort of eerie and sinister undertone that would also conjure up images of another one-gloved villain, Freddy, who is so formative to the genre."

—JORDAN PEELE

SONY

CHAPTER 6

JUST AN ITSY-BITSY THING

Once the Wilsons set foot on the boardwalk in Santa Cruz, Adelaide spots a familiar sight—the Shaman's Vision Quest from her childhood, except the attraction has since been rebranded as Merlin's Forest. Whether this is the deliberate erasure of a large group of Americans or simply an attempt to correct what some may have seen as stereotypical imagery, the Indigenous chief has been replaced with a stone-faced wizard, still pointing and promising that, inside, patrons will find themselves.

Merlin's Forest harkens back to European medieval mythology, in which the forest of Brocéliande, where the Arthurian wizard was imprisoned, is a place of magic, mystery, and danger. In some iterations of the story, the forest includes the Vale (or Valley) of No Return, where people become imprisoned by tree branches, and a lake, the Fair Mirror, where fairies would admire reflections of themselves.

We soon are introduced to Josh Tyler, Gabe's colleague from work, and his wife, Kitty. The two appear to be the model American couple—white, married, and affluent—but when one looks closer, Peele suggests through Kym Barrett's costume designs that there may be more to the Tylers than meets the eye. Take, for example, Kitty's golden-frame sunglasses: Instead of being appropriately tinted to protect from the sun, the lenses are pink—for the superficial, fashion trumps function. Through Kitty's privileged eyes, the world is rose-tinted.

In contrast, Adelaide's sunglasses are dark. Her primary goal is protection, and she sees the world as grimmer. The differences in their eyewear highlights the dissimilarity between the two women and how they see the world.

"The Tylers are Gabe's best friends, but not his family's best friends," Winston Duke says. "Gabe's friendship with Josh Tyler is a reflection of Gabe's deep need to have an attachment or proximity to what he views as potential perfection. Gabe thinks the Tylers'

OPPOSITE: The frisbee that oddly and coincidentally lands on Adelaide's beach blanket.
ABOVE: Elisabeth Moss as Kitty on the beach.

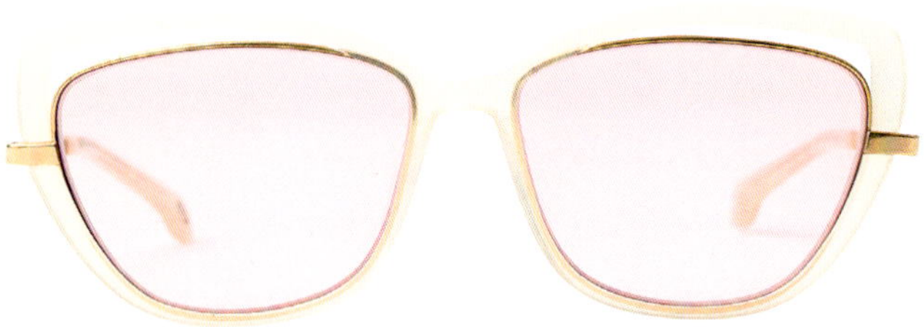

family is perfect. They're this white, rich, upper-middle-class family, and Gabe wants to hang out with them because he thinks it will rub off on him and his own family. In that relationship, though, the Tylers can be a bit condescending, and it might not be very healthy for Gabe and his family, long term."

Josh is played by Tim Heidecker, who caught the eye of Peele after starring in the 2012 film *The Comedy*. "In that film, Tim nails the presumptuous sourness of the straight-white-American-male trope, but he does it in a way that somehow manages to inspire empathy," *Us* producer Ian Cooper says. "It's a truly grotesque character, but Tim carves the character into something so multidimensional you can't just vilify him."

"Jordan joked that *The Comedy* was essentially Tim's audition for the role of Josh," he adds.

For Kitty, Peele turned to Golden Globe winner Elisabeth Moss, best known to audiences for her starring roles in *Mad Men* and *The Handmaid's Tale*. Like Heidecker, Moss emerged as an early favorite in the casting process. Cooper encouraged Peele to consider her for the role, largely based on her role in the 2013 BBC miniseries *Top of the Lake*. When she and Peele met to discuss *Us*, she agreed to the part, sight unseen. "I was like, 'I don't want to sound desperate, but 'yes,'" she says. "He said, 'Well, I'll send the script to you, and you can let me know what you think,' and I was like, 'I don't think you understand. I'm serious. Whatever it is, I'll do it.'"

"Lizzie does amazing things in the film," Peele says. "She has such refined tools as an actor. She'll give you a take that's so beautiful and nuanced and intentionally off-balance, and then you ask her to try it another way, and she'll give you a take that is just as brilliant and entirely different. She really brought a fourth dimension to the character of Kitty and cemented who she was."

We next meet Becca and Lindsey Tyler, Josh and Kitty's twin daughters, played by Cali and Noelle Sheldon, who began their acting careers as infants sharing the role of Ross and Rachel's daughter, Emma, on *Friends*.

When we first see them, Becca is wearing a pink-and-blue bikini top and blue denim cutoff shorts. She looks very California beach chic, while her sister stands in contrast in dark denim cutoffs and a tank top with the logo for the punk band Black Flag.

TOP: Kitty's rose-colored glasses.
ABOVE: Zora in conversation with Becca and Lindsey Tyler, played by Cali and Noelle Sheldon.

ON THIS PAGE: The Tyler twins and Zora's t-shirts.

M

OPPOSITE: Jordan Peele and Lupita Nyong'o on set at the Merlin Forest's sinister underbelly.
TOP: The final set build for the exterior of Merlin's Forest. **ABOVE:** The pre-build detailed rendering for Merlin's Forest.

Interestingly, this isn't the first Black Flag shirt to appear in *Us*. At the Santa Cruz boardwalk in 1986, the Whac-A-Mole worker wears a shirt with the album art for the band's 1984 *My War* album. The key image is of a hand puppet with a red body—essentially, a lone glove—wielding a knife. It's another image the observant Addy files away in her memory.

Of course, when it comes to war, white flags are associated with surrender. By extension, a black flag would represent the inverse—no surrender.

Throughout *Us*, graphic T-shirts are used to highlight the film's key themes and influences. For example, Jason wears a baseball shirt emblazoned with the logo for the 1975 film *Jaws* to the beach. The Steven Spielberg movie introduced terror to a generation, with the shark acting as a monster that lives beneath the surface and pulls unsuspecting people under. Individuals enjoy their lives, blissfully unaware that a deadly threat is ready to strike when given the chance.

Just as Alfred Hitchcock made moviegoers afraid of showers in 1960, Steven Spielberg transformed the beach into a location for potential terror. Peele embraced the opportunity to continue the legacy of using the shoreline as a setting for cinematic horror. "The beach itself conjures up this high-low tension contrast," Ian Cooper says. "You've got the romantic splendor of the landscape—sand meeting ocean—and simultaneously, the sweaty, seedy underbelly vibes of what goes on at a beachfront boardwalk."

TOP: Jason's Jaws t-shirt.
BOTTOM: A frisbee with a shooting star emblem lands on a towel in front of Adelaide and Kitty.

"Horror movies that take place in dark, dusty, muddy houses or basements—it's kind of like, 'yeah, what do you expect,'" Peele says. "But the horror movies that take place in idyllic environments, *The Stepford Wives*, *Jaws*, even *The Shining*? The horror you can get from daylight, and places that are supposed to be vacation, I think they're scarier.

"There's a more satirical horror to them, but also they kind of give the audience their cake and they get to eat it too," he continues. "They get to go on adventure, or a vacation, as opposed to being claustrophobic."

While Adelaide and Kitty are talking, an errant Frisbee—red, with a gold star—lands on the beach blanket in front of them. These two colors will have greater significance later in the film. Also, it is customary in many cultures to make a wish on a descending star, and some cultures believe that the celestial occurrence is a sign that a soul is being reborn on Earth. The Chinese philosopher Confucius stated that shooting stars are visual evidence of souls passing either to heaven or the underworld.

When the Frisbee lands, it perfectly covers a blue dot on the blanket. The standard is replaced by the deviation, as if it were always meant to be there.

After a visit to the Port-A-Shell portable toilet, Jason sees on the beach an unusual figure with outstretched arms and a long, green jacket almost covering a red jumpsuit that peeks out underneath. The man's fingertips—one set gloved—drip with blood.

Jason wanders back toward his panicked mother, who believes she's lost him, not knowing he has just seen one of the Tethered.

TOP: The custom design for the Santa Cruz Boardwalk's Port-A-Shell bathroom signage.
ABOVE: Jason comes upon one of the Tethered.

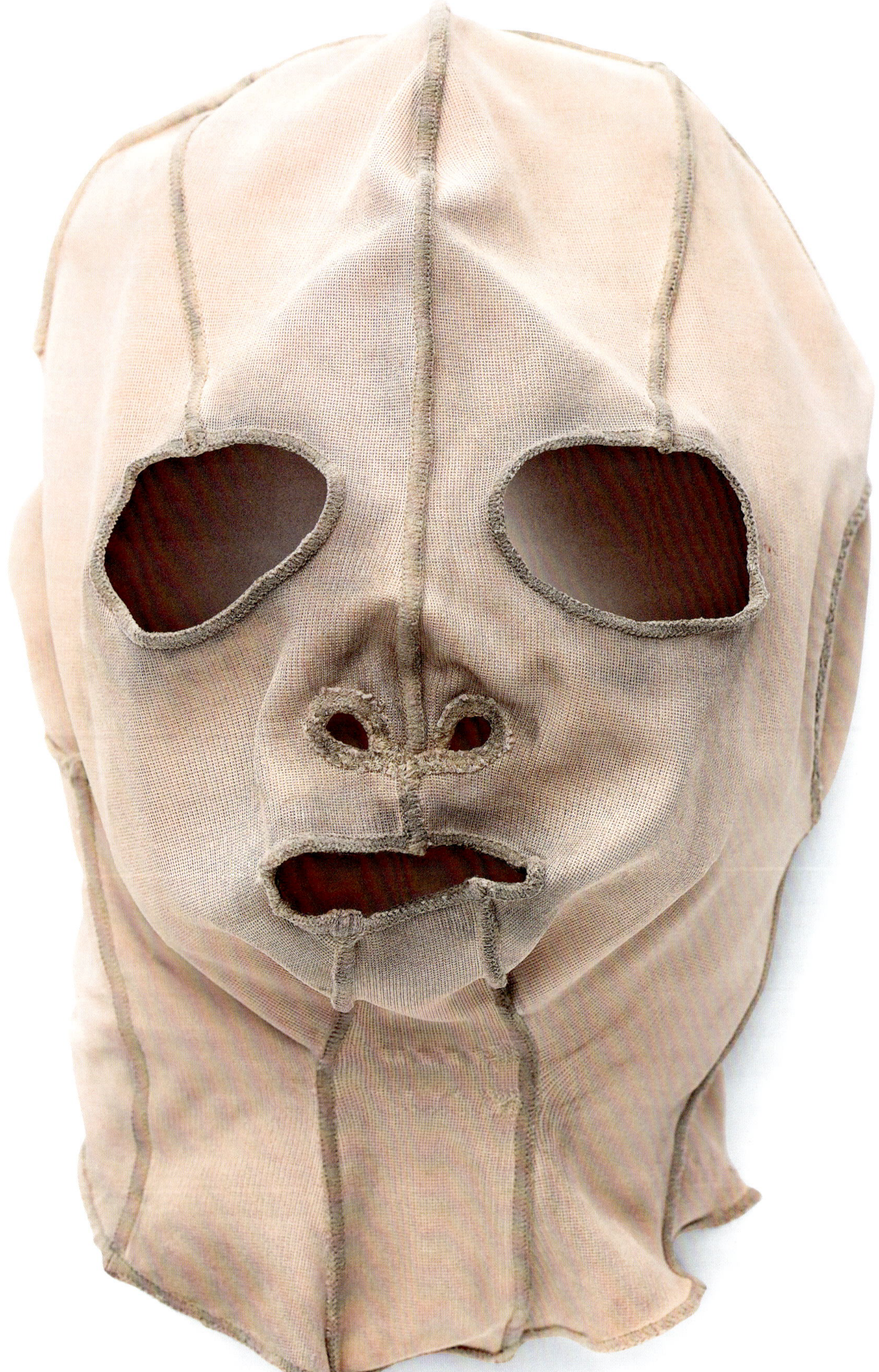

CHAPTER 7

WE'RE AMERICANS

The family returns to their vacation home and prepares to settle in for the night. Adelaide and Jason share a quiet moment, reflecting on what occurred at the beach, when he notices that the clock reads 11:11. Adelaide's face telegraphs her unease. This is the same number that appeared on the strange man's cardboard sign, and moments earlier, she overheard that 11–11 was the score of the basketball game Gabe was watching—all coincidences, but perhaps also a harbinger of something negative on the horizon.

Just as she seems poised to push these strange occurrences aside, Adelaide spots a drawing on the dresser in Jason's bedroom. It's a pseudo-self-portrait, a child's illustration of the back of Jason's own head, looking at the back of the person in a green jacket, single-gloved, with bloody fingertips. In the background, the sun, adjacent to amusement park rides and palm trees, beams brightly. The image is both light and dark, innocent and adult. As the viewers, we are looking at Adelaide looking at Jason looking at the unidentified man, a cycle of faceless voyeurism.

OPPOSITE: Pluto's mask, which conceals his secret scars.
ABOVE: Adelaide studies Jason's artwork after their Santa Cruz beach trip.

"The choice to put Adelaide in sisterlocks is particularly great," Peele says. "I can't remember seeing a central character in a film wearing sisterlocks, and that alone is an important piece of film history—to see real Black women's hairstyles on film in lead roles."

Adelaide tries to convince Gabe to leave the vacation home by telling him she's feeling uneasy, haunted by having seen a doppelgänger at the boardwalk as a child. It's clear that her husband doesn't believe her, and before their conversation can properly conclude, for the second time in the film, the power goes out. Jason arrives in their bedroom to share some startling news: "There's a family in our driveway."

Gabe, ignoring his wife's advice to remain in the house, steps out to confront the four individuals. Despite Gabe "asking them nice" to leave, the four remain, unmoving, almost in silhouette. It's impossible to make out their faces or clothing, but it's clear that their hands are linked—tethered—while they stand in the darkness as an overhead light shines brightly behind them.

Jason sits up in bed, playing with his magic ring. His pajama top, fittingly, is a long-sleeved white pajama T-shirt with a printed image of a tuxedo jacket's lapel, a ruffled dress shirt, and a black bowtie. The faux formal wear highlights an unspoken aspect of Jason's character. "Jason was a magician," costume designer Kym Barrett says. "He can see beyond, or he can see through, the veil."

"I feel like you can imagine him in his pajamas, doing his magic tricks in front of the mirror," she continues. "The mirror is a gateway to another world in horror movies. It's often a gateway to the next dimension, or a side-by-side reality."

A few moments later, in the master bedroom, we see Gabe's sleepwear, a gray Howard University sweatshirt. Founded in 1867, Howard is one of the United States' historically Black universities, with a longstanding mission of uplifting traditionally marginalized communities. According to its website, "The University has long held a commitment to the study of disadvantaged persons in American society and throughout the world. The goal is the elimination of inequalities related to race, color, social, economic, and political circumstances."

Racial identity and cultural history are reflected in Gabe's clothing, just as it is reflected in Adelaide's hair. Camille Friend and Lupita Nyong'o worked closely together to develop a style for the character that would be simultaneously contemporary and grounded in Adelaide's familial and cultural roots. "We came up with the sisterlock [hairstyle] because she wanted to do something that was natural," Friend says. "We're always trying to push the envelope and do things that are different, even within the natural [hair] genre. It represents her as a woman. It's really modern and what people are doing now."

TOP: Jason's tuxedo pajamas.
ABOVE: The mysterious Tethered family in the Wilsons' driveway.

The patriarch returns inside and, after learning the police are fourteen minutes away, he retrieves a metal baseball bat. This will be his makeshift weapon, like a club, an instrument primal in nature—and, in the right hands, an effective defense tool.

But before he has a chance to swing, the members of the "bad family" unlock themselves from each other. The children race into the foliage, while the largest adult lumbers toward the house. The father retreats inside to his family, and together, they are captives in a home designed to protect them.

Outside, the final remaining "bad adult" makes their way down the driveway while whistling "The Itsy-Bitsy Spider," a curiously familiar tune. The figure bends down to pick up a rock. It appears that it will be used as a tool to enter the house through brute force, but once the rock is turned over, we see that it is an artifice—a Hide-a-Key. In a sense, it is a magic trick, although, unlike Jason's futile attempts at making his ring spark, this one is successful—in the worst way.

The door is unlocked, the windows are smashed in, and within moments, the Wilsons find themselves face-to-face with the "bad family." When the youngest intruder ignites the fireplace, the Wilsons (and the viewers) see their faces for the first time—that is, with the notable exception of the youngest, who is wearing a mask that covers his entire head.

Three of the Wilsons struggle to make sense of what they're seeing. Jason knows.

"It's us."

Red, Adelaide's doppelgänger, soon answers alternatively, "We're Americans."

Once Adelaide and Red are alone together, Red recounts a story of a girl and her shadow. The two lived parallel lives—when they ate, when they received gifts, who they fell in love with, and when they gave

TOP: Gabe arms himself with a baseball bat to defend his family.
ABOVE: The Hide-a-Key that fails to protect the Wilsons' home from the invasion.

GOOD FAMILY *VERSUS* BAD FAMILY

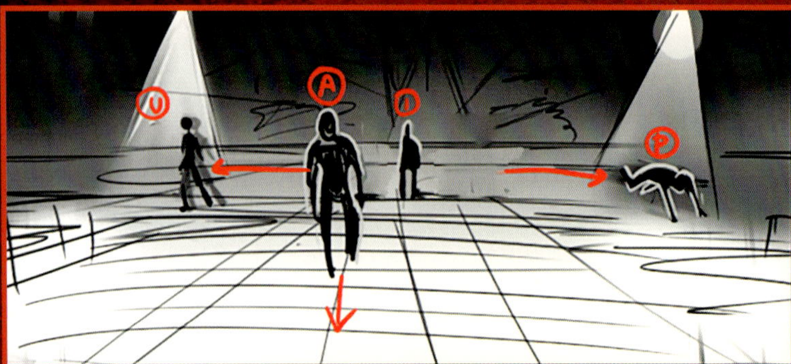

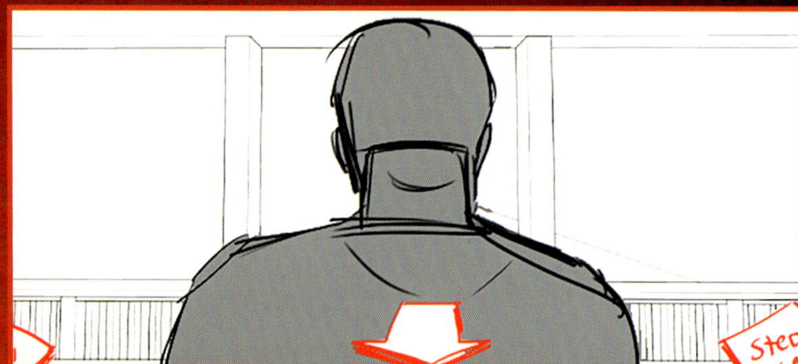

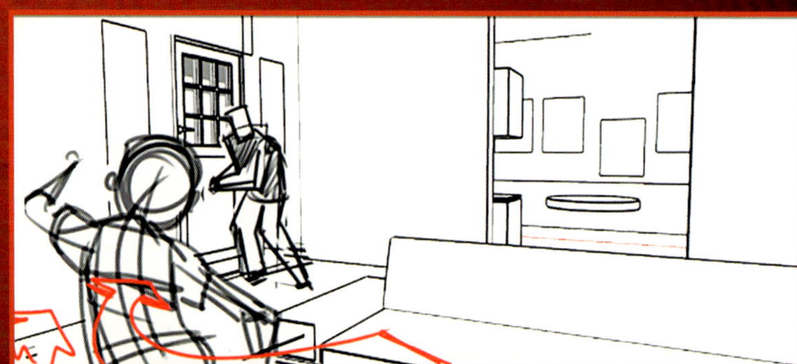

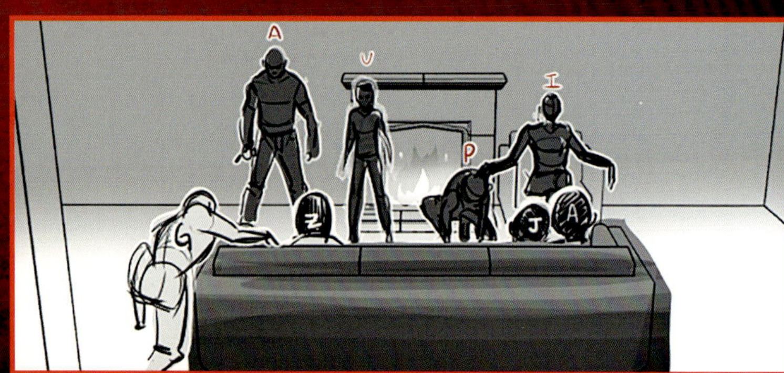

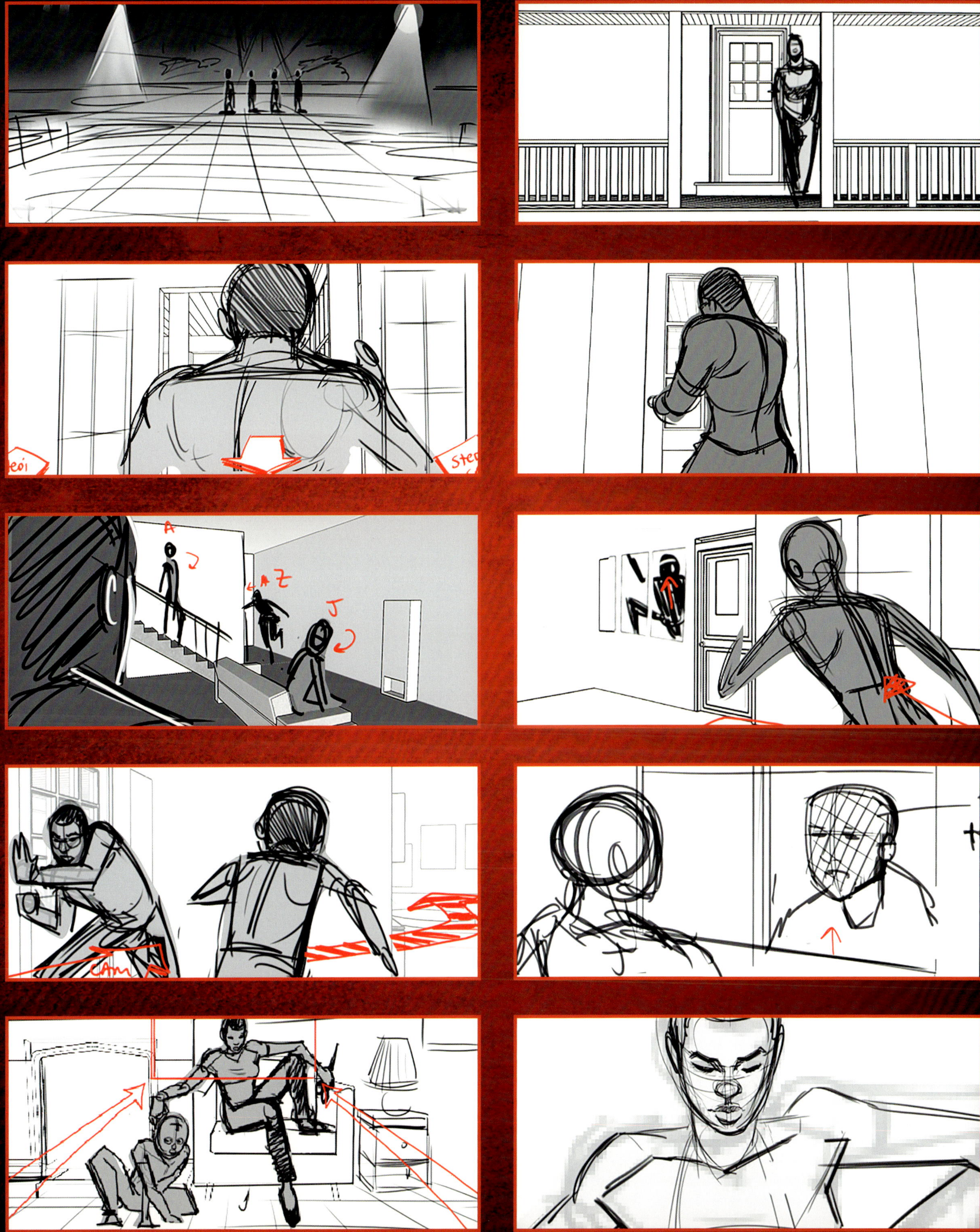
A
J
CAM

"I had always envisioned the Tethered as a violent cult, and the fact that their uniform communicates it unanimously and that image on the driveway illuminates their intentions, methods, and the desires of their reckoning is what I found so special."

—JORDAN PEELE

birth—but the girl's was significantly more charmed. Although they were intertwined, for every beautiful moment the girl experienced, the shadow lived a horror. This sparked the shadow's hatred for the girl until the day she realized she was being tested by God.

Red orders Adelaide to tether herself to the coffee table using a pair of handcuffs provided by Pluto, Jason's doppelgänger. Handcuffs are instruments of both bondage and servitude, and once Adelaide submits to Red's plans, they serve as a physical symbol that the family's matriarch has lost control of both the situation and her position. Structurally, handcuffs are one physical pair, connected together by a simple chain that possesses immense strength—that is, until the bond is broken.

As Adelaide complies with Red's demand, Abraham, Gabe's tethered counterpart, tries on Gabe's glasses. For the first time, the shadow experiences a moment of privilege. "Abraham is really a partner to Red," Winston Duke says. "He's there to make sure everything works. He's there to make sure everything is achieved. And because he doesn't have great eyesight, he has to listen. He has to be present, even more than Gabe is."

Abraham strikes Gabe in the knee with the baseball bat before dragging him across shards of the broken window toward the front door. Umbrae, Zora's double, a wide grin taking up the bottom half of her face, emerges to confront her counterpart. "Umbrae is probably the scariest one in the bunch, for me personally," Peele says. "She has this creepy smile, and she's weirdly obsessed with

PAGES 74–75: Storyboards for the Tethered's invasion of the Wilson house. **PREVIOUS SPREAD:** Red tells her tale. **TOP:** Red wields her scissors in the Wilson sitting room. **ABOVE:** The handcuffs Red uses to tether Adelaide to the coffee table.

TOP AND ABOVE LEFT: Jason, Zora, and Gabe listen to Red's story.
ABOVE RIGHT: Filming the home invasion sequence.

Zora in almost a respectful way, even though she's going to try to kill her. Umbrae holds a lot of menace and may be my favorite character in the movie."

On Red's command, and with Adelaide's encouragement, the older Wilson child runs out of the house. Her shadow, appropriately, remains close behind.

Jason and Pluto go into the hallway closet to "play," with Adelaide quietly telling her son to show his doppelgänger a magic trick. As he did earlier that day, Jason leaves a toy ambulance wedged in the door frame to prevent being locked inside. It's a curious plaything—childlike and playful while also evoking injury and the potential for death.

Back at the fireplace, Red has confronted the paralyzed Adelaide, the prey caught in the spider's web. The doppelgänger pushes her counterpart's head into the coffee table, against the glass surface, which begins to fracture under the pressure. Once again, Peele has crafted a masterful shot. Although glass is meant to be seen through, in this moment, the pane acts as a mirror. Adelaide's face is pressed into the glass, and we see her reflection—but also, we see Red. As Red begins to share details of the Untethering, her plan for the people of the underground to reclaim their place as Americans, Adelaide's "shadow" is the only figure with complete autonomy.

"When Lupita was playing Red, something entirely different happened," Peele says. "She would walk into the room and you could just feel it sort of ice over. She has this amazing anticipatory presence in that character, and you just know within moments of meeting her that she holds all the cards."

While Red is tending to Adelaide, Abraham has put his double inside a trash bag aboard the *Craw Daddy*, Gabe's ramshackle speedboat. This leads to a visually arresting fight between the two men, the first sequence Eric Yamamoto storyboarded for *Us*. "The boat sequence was challenging for a lot of people to wrap their head around, because filming water at night is incredibly challenging," Yamamoto says. "Jordan had pretty much everything in mind, in terms of what the scene should look like. We just sat down and just started to play with ideas."

TOP AND ABOVE RIGHT: Jason's toy ambulance. **ABOVE LEFT:** Jordan Peele prepares to film with Evan Alex and his stand-in. **OPPOSITE:** Storyboards of the sequence where Umbrae hunts Zora.

ZORA
VERSUS
UMBRAE

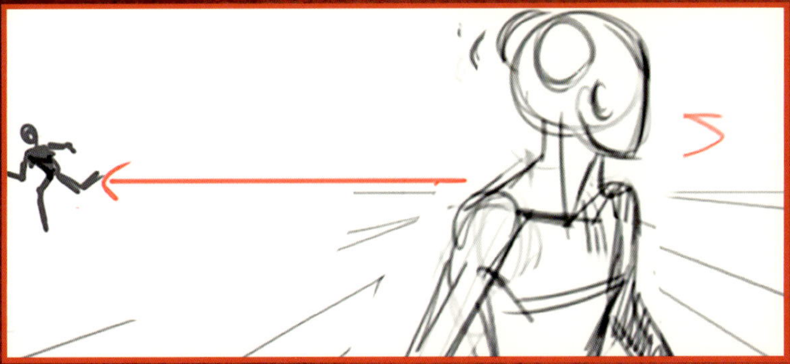

MAGIC

GABE *VERSUS* ABRAHAM

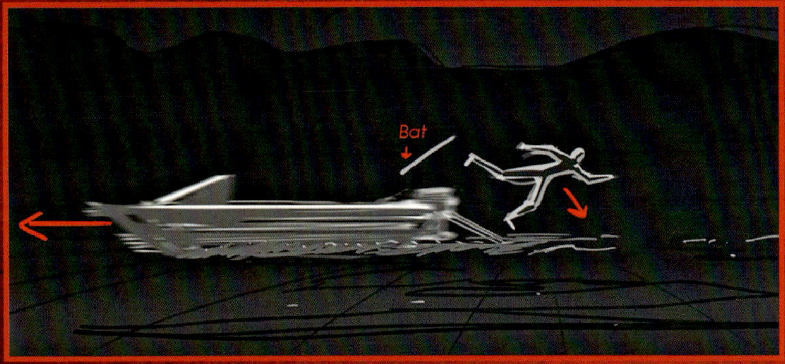

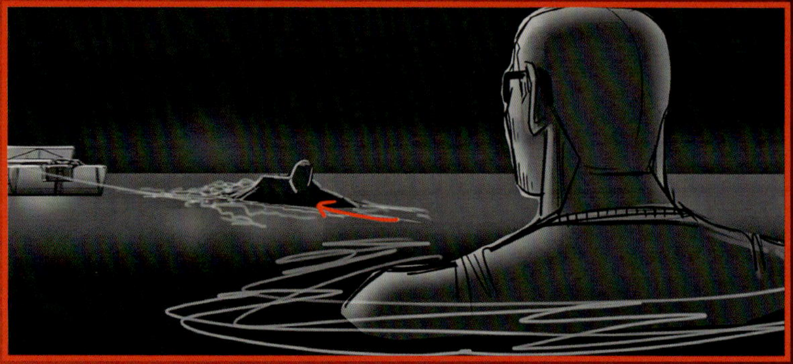

While Yamamoto was collaborating with Peele on how the scene would look in the finished film, there was a pivotal moment that helped clarify the lengths and limitations of the Tethereds' abilities. "I didn't understand what the doppelgängers were," Yamamoto continues. "Jordan wanted the 'bad dad' to stop a baseball bat that was swinging at him with his hand. I was like, 'Oh, so they kind of have superpowers,' and Jordan said, 'No, no, no. They're determined.'"

Within the construct of the film, Adelaide is as determined as her doppelgänger. One of the clearest examples of her desire to survive and protect her family is in the initial home-invasion sequence, after she's been left alone, tethered to the coffee table. Red has gone to check on Pluto, who, moments earlier, screamed in fear after Jason's magic ring successfully created a spark. For Adelaide, fire isn't a source of fear or fascination—it's a path to freedom.

She takes note of the long metal poker next to the fireplace. The instrument is designed to be used at arm's length when building a fire, but frustratingly, it is just out of her reach. Finally, her dancer's instincts kick in. She uses her foot to pick up the tool—demonstrating her ability to think creatively and survive by any means necessary—and uses the poker to break the coffee table's wooden leg, to which she's handcuffed. She is partially freed—able to leave the living room, even though her hands are still tethered together.

Within a few moments, the Wilson family is reunited. Adelaide has found Jason and taken him outside, with Pluto following behind in hot pursuit. Zora has returned home, having escaped from Umbrae. Gabe has won his fight with Abraham, regained control of the *Craw Daddy*, and returned to the dock to retrieve his family.

The Wilsons escape, believing they will find safety on the other side of the lake. Red, Umbrae, and Pluto remain behind, plotting their next move.

In the distance, the Tylers are also enjoying a quiet moment within the safety of their home. Unbeknownst to them, their Tethered counterparts are plotting too.

PREVIOUS SPREAD: Jason and Pluto. **OPPOSTE:** Storyboards of the fight sequence between Gabe and Abraham. **TOP:** A tethered Adelaide weighs her options. **ABOVE:** Gabe's baseball bat.

CHAPTER 8

SHE WASN'T A REFLECTION

The home-invasion sequence is the first time audiences see the Tethered, the self-described "Americans" who live in underground tunnels and barracks, who are "shadow" doubles of those living freely above. Each wears a matching uniform, which is as functional as it is menacing.

In designing the Tethereds' signature look, costume designer Kym Barrett worked closely with Peele and production designer Ruth De Jong. "The look of the Tethered was probably the most important design choice we made in this film, because that is our monster," Peele says. "A lot of thought went into those decisions. I wanted to create an iconic look that utilized grounded elements. I didn't want anything too fantastical or over the top. I wanted to allow them to be people."

"When I started, there were still a lot of options. They'd explored a couple of them, but ultimately, they just couldn't make the costumes fit properly," Barrett says. "We had a lot of discussions about the context of the Tethered, where they resided in time and space, and what was it like to be born in the underworld, knowing that you were a shadow of another part of you. There was a lot of psychological discussion in trying to work out how we represent these ideas without beating people over the head."

OPPOSITE: One of The Tethereds' signature coveralls.
ABOVE: Adelaide face-to-face with The Tethered.

While studying the script and brainstorming ways to best execute Peele's vision, Barrett envisioned the Tethered as having a simple silhouette. One of her first ideas that caught on was to put the doppelgängers in Cold War–era uniforms. "I started researching vintage work wear," Barrett says. "There had to be a uniformity to what they wore, a utilitarian work-wear component. We knew that they had an ideologically intense mentality."

However, that idea came and went. With only two weeks to settle on a final look, Barrett continued to consider the concept of uniformity. The answer, she soon realized, was clothing the Tethered in coveralls. "It was kind of an obvious choice," she says. "It's very cultlike, and I thought, a man or woman could wear it, a small or big person could wear it. They could all have the same uniform look."

"Coveralls also evoked mass factories, mass munitions, like a Communist army," she adds. "We were building an army of the Tethered."

From the beginning of the process, Peele knew he wanted the doppelgängers to be dressed in red. "Red has so many deep ancient resonances," Barrett says. "Think about *Carrie*. There are lot of very iconic movies where people become drenched in blood, or are figuratively drenched in their own blood. It's like when people put leeches on themselves as an expulsion of evil. Blood is in a lot of witchcraft, and potions, and all kinds of cultural and shamanistic rituals."

"Just the idea of being able to utilize a flash of red going by in the darkness to signify your monster was exciting, and it carries with it this connotation of an escaped prisoner or patient," Peele says. "It's also a kind of an allusion to classic horror characters like Michael Myers and Freddy Krueger."

Besides *Halloween* and *A Nightmare on Elm Street* being seminal horror films, formative for Peele's filmmaking career, these films were also integral sources of inspiration for the Tethered within the narrative of *Us*. "Red is sort of culturally paused in 1986," Ian Cooper says. "So her wardrobe references are things like Michael Jackson's "Thriller," Michael Myers' jumpsuit from *Halloween*, Freddy Kruger's bladed glove. Kym really saw eye-to-eye with us on that and was down to take big-swing risks."

Both Michael Jackson and Freddy Kruger inspired the idea of the Tethered each wearing a single leather glove, which protects the doppelgängers' hands when they are wielding their large and lethal golden scissors. In their hands, the otherwise-mundane

TOP: One of The Tethereds' lone leather gloves.
ABOVE: Adelaide prepares to take down Red in the Underpass.

ON THIS PAGE: Kym Barrett's costume designs for Gabe and Adelaide in their beachwear, and their Tethered counterparts.

ON THIS PAGE: Kym Barrett's costume designs for Zora and Jason and their doppelgangers.

household implements are brutal weapons and, like most aspects of *Us*, connect to the film's main theme. Scissors consist of two mirror components, containing elements of both union and separation. They are a symbol of duality—inextricably connected—with both parts functioning as one.

The Tethereds' coveralls have shortened sleeves, allowing audiences to see the blood on their hands, and pants hemmed above the ankle. To complete the look, Barrett put each doppelgänger in flat, tan sandals. "I felt that added a kind of monastic, religious element to them," she says. "Sandals are, again, very utilitarian. You always see acolytes in Bible stories, like Jesus, wearing sandals. Cults tend to live in more pastoral settings, like in Hawaii, Costa Rica, or California. We decided we wanted that cult feeling of giving up everything for the ultimate aim of the group."

As the costumes were being decided, makeup designer Scott Wheeler created the specific look for each member of the Wilson family. "Typically in a movie that involves doppelgängers, there's a gag where you think one doppelgänger is the other," he says. "Jordan said no to that. He wanted the doppelgängers to look really different than their counterparts because they've lived different lives."

According to Wheeler, Peele wanted the Tethered to look like "subtle vampires." To achieve the desired effect, the makeup artist made each actor's skin appear pale and gray. Lupita Nyong'o came up with the idea to bleach Red's eyebrows so they appeared as if they had been accidentally burned off by Pluto, Jason's doppelgänger. To avoid the risk of doing permanent damage to her eyebrows, Wheeler collaborated with her makeup artist, Shutchai Tym Buacharern, to achieve the look with special effects mascara. Buacharern backcombed Nyong'o's now-blonde brows for a finishing touch, making them appear as if they had truly been singed.

While the eyebrow look was designed specifically for Red, the result was so effective that it was applied, to varying degrees, to all the Tethered.

Camille Friend designed hairstyles for each of the Wilsons' doppelgängers, which also deviated significantly from the way their aboveground counterparts appeared. "A lot of what makes the Tethered the Tethered is their hair," Peele says. By way of example, Friend wanted both Red and Adelaide to have the same hair texture but appear stylistically different. Because Red would have been underground without access to beauty tools and products, Friend left her hair in thick, natural curls.

The look for Gabe's doppelgänger, Abraham, required that hair extensions be applied to Winston Duke's face before filming each day in order to achieve a more rugged and rustic look. "There tended to be a little less personal care involved in the look of the doppelgängers," Scott Wheeler says. "We played them a bit more proletariat. Winston Duke's character, Gabe, for instance, has a nicely groomed beard. His doppelgänger just has this biblical beard that he's let grow out. We did that with a hand-laid beard, and we really pushed the limits of shadow and highlight on his face to reshape his face."

To mirror Jason's werewolf mask, Pluto, his Tethered counterpart, has a face covering of his own. However, beneath his doppelgänger's lies a secret—an expansive scar, presumably caused by Pluto burning himself while playing with fire. To achieve the effect, a prosthetic was put on Evan Alex's face for scenes in which he portrays Pluto. "At first Jordan wanted it to look as if Pluto had endured small burns over the course of his life, but then he decided, no, the scar was going to be the result of one big burn," Wheeler says. "And that's kind of the monster of the movie."

TOP: The Tethered recreate Hands Across America.
ABOVE: The Tethereds' signature sandal footwear.

CHAPTER 9

GOOD VIBRATIONS

In contrast to the Wilsons' cozy abode, the Tylers live in a house that mirrors who they are—beautiful, yet empty and cold. Once again, character was a key factor in selecting the right home.

"The Tyler house also required a lot of scouting," production designer Ruth De Jong says. "We wanted it to be very contemporary, and a big juxtaposition to the Wilson house. But we had the same challenges that we did with finding the Wilson house. We ended up finding a fantastic place in Calabasas. The topography of the yard was perfect. It was very private, and it gave the illusion that the boat dock was just out of sight.

"The difference visually between these two families and their homes is quite obvious, I hope," she says. "The Wilsons' home was inherited whereas the Tylers' was a second home. It was somewhat of a 'keeping up with the Joneses' situation. The house they inherited was outside of their means, whereas the Tylers' had the money to live this fancy, contemporary nouveau riche lifestyle. They didn't have taste, per se, but they had money which allowed for their fancy boat, Land Rover, and second home at the beach."

Audiences are treated to a full view of the home during a sequence that Peele has referred to as the "seven-second massacre," wherein the Tylers' doppelgängers slaughter the entire family in just a few moments. As their shadows are untethering themselves from the Tylers, Peele expertly opts to take his viewers outside for an equally disconnected view of the action. We are voyeurs as Josh, Kitty, Becca, and Lindsey fall victim to the Tethereds' lethal scissors, while The Beach Boys' 1967 hit "Good Vibrations" provides the soundtrack to the carnage.

OPPOSITE: The bloodied geode in the Tyler home.
ABOVE: The Tyler home, post-massacre, with the Ophelia home assistant prominently featured.

The ironic music choice is playing throughout the house on "Ophelia," a fictional artificial intelligence home-assistance device. Throughout the 2010s, similar devices such as Amazon's Alexa rose in popularity around the world. With a few simple verbal commands, these computerized aids can play music, make telephone calls, order food, and perform a number of other household functions to make life easier for the humans seemingly in control.

However, just as Peele has done throughout *Us*, Ophelia serves as a reminder of the pitfalls of modernity. Just like the Hide-a-Key, other gadgets designed to make our lives easier may ultimately contribute to our downfall. Ophelia's failings throughout this scene, particularly when Kitty commands it to "Call the police!" and it responds by blasting N.W.A.'s 1988 anthem "Fuck Tha Police," illustrate how money cannot buy safety. It's a deeply anticapitalist critique, and a commentary on prioritizing convenient solutions.

In some ways, Ophelia's inadequacies—or, perhaps, her defiance—could have been predicted. The device's name harkens back to William Shakespeare's *Hamlet*, wherein the character of Ophelia is defined by her relationships with her lover, her brother, and her father. Like her namesake in *Us*, Ophelia is given little agency or independent identity. She is expected to respond to every command, and eventually, it drives her mad.

Once again, popular music is used to expert effect. "Fuck Tha Police" is an inspired song choice. Beyond its comedic value, Peele encourages us to consider the song's lyrics—"comin' straight from the underground"—and its decades-long history of being used to protest American inequality and challenge the role of law enforcement. Earlier in *Us*, Adelaide called the police when the mysterious family was in her driveway, but they never arrived. Kitty's cries for help also go unanswered, at least in the way she anticipated. Later in this sequence, Adelaide can't get through to the police on the phone at all. "How does 911 keep you on hold all night long?" Gabe asks. "I just don't get it."

Such institutions, it seems, are fallible in a moment of true crisis.

Interestingly, there were alternative song choices on the table in postproduction. "Jordan likes to explore the different possibilities," composer Michael Abels says. "I've seen versions of the scene with 'Fuck Tha Police,' and there was at least one other version with a Police song," he adds, referring to the band's 1978 single "Roxanne."

TOP: The balcony inside the Tyler home.
ABOVE: Becca and Lindsey fall victim to their Tethered counterparts in a matter of seconds.

"It was the same joke, but it had a very different vibe to the scene," Abels continues. "It was clever, but 'Fuck Tha Police' is in your face. I'm personally glad that it was that song. It was clearly the right choice."

Once the Wilsons arrive at the Tylers' home, the threat in *Us* heightens: Our protagonists discover that the Tethered aren't limited to their own doppelgängers, and the Wilsons are confronted with another "bad family."

Adelaide uses the poker that freed her, which she's brought along for protection, to kill Tex, Josh's double. Zora, meanwhile, finds her own weapon of choice—a golf club, an instrument historically associated with the social elite. It's a symbol of American exclusivity, designed for precise movements. In Zora's hands, it's a blunt object of destruction.

Jason arms himself with a geode, a physical manifestation of beauty turned inside out—and a reminder that one person's ornament is another's weapon. And unlike a poker, a golf club, or a baseball bat, the object has to be employed with a strong, direct blow from within close range for the object to do damage.

Beauty is also on display immediately after Zora and Jason seemingly kill Nix, Lindsey Tyler's doppelgänger. Kitty's double, Dahlia, is seated at the vanity in the master bedroom, applying makeup. Like her counterpart, she is infatuated with her looks. "Kitty is, in some ways, a modern-day Marilyn Monroe who never got the chance to become an actress," costume designer Kym Barrett says. "She's living in her own imagination of what she thinks a mother should be and what she wishes she could've done with her life."

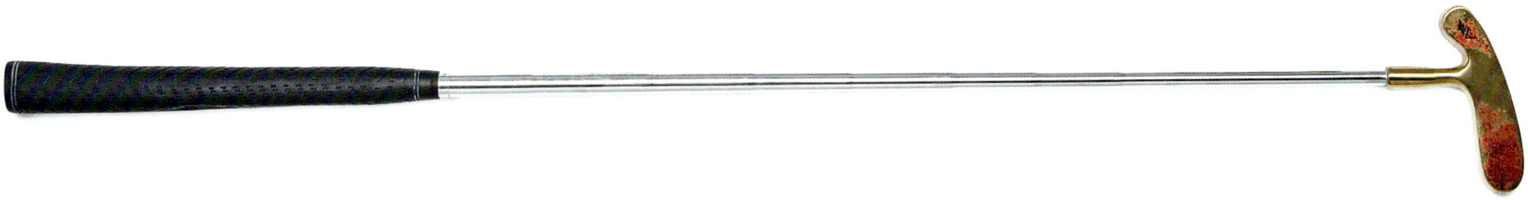

TOP: Jason grabs the geode for protection.
ABOVE: The fatal golfclub.

With a wide smile and her eyes transfixed on her reflection in the mirror, Dahlia puts her scissors to her cheekbone and drags them toward her chin. As the blood runs down her face, she never breaks her stare. Earlier, on the beach, Kitty confessed to having gotten an "itsy-bitsy" amount of plastic surgery; Dahlia has taken the concept to extreme, grotesque lengths, although in her eyes, she is beautiful.

Outside the Tyler house, Gabe has lured Tex onto the *B-Yacht'ch*, Josh's speedboat. Peele places both families' boats in the same frame. It is clear that the Tylers' vehicle is superior in size—and it will soon be revealed, to Gabe's benefit, that it also surpasses the *Craw Daddy* in amenities.

Gabe hides within the darkness of the boat, and when Tex is within close range, he fires an Orion-brand flare gun at him. The moment is a pay-off for an exchange earlier in the film, when Josh notes to Gabe that the *Craw Daddy* lacks this specific "essential" item.

While the flare gun, discharging a blast of bright light and smoke, is useful in creating a distress signal, it makes for a subpar weapon. There is an irony, then, that it is named after Orion, a mighty hunter in Greek mythology. True to form, the flare gun does little to stop Tex, and the two men get into a brawl on the boat. Luckily, Gabe is the victor.

Once Gabe returns to the house, the Wilson family unit is once again complete. However, the quartet learn through the television news that countless doppelgängers are wreaking havoc throughout the United States. Adelaide, appointing herself decision-maker, instructs her family to get into the Tylers' car. They're outside when Adelaide realizes she's forgotten the keys, and when she goes back in the Tyler home to retrieve them, she is attacked by a bloodied, feral Nix.

Adelaide spots a pair of golden scissors, and with the deftness of the Tethered themselves, she finishes Nix off. Jason reenters the home just in time to see his mother commit a violent murder, and alongside him, we notice the stark change in the color of her pajamas: Her once-white top is considerably bloodied. She is becoming transformed, just as she has been evolving throughout *Us*.

"Leading up to the white look, Adelaide was in pale pink, pale blue, pale yellow—creamy colors," Kym Barrett says. "I wanted there to be a progression towards white. Then I wanted the evolution in the amount of blood on her clothing to be the bridge between her normal half and her Tethered half, so that she was progressively becoming, acknowledging, and fully encompassing the Tethered part of herself."

Of course, the blood in this scene wasn't limited to being seen only on Adelaide's costume. The "Seven-Second Massacre" is the goriest in *Us*, which created a logistical problem easily solved by visual effects supervisor Grady Cofer of Industrial Light & Magic (ILM). "The house that was chosen for this location had a pristine white carpet," he says. "No one relished the idea of having four blood bags bursting in that environment." Instead, the blood was digitally added in postproduction.

However, when Peele did need to represent pools of blood, the effects team came up with a different creative solution. "They created these blood mats that are rubber, but look like they're liquid," Ruth De Jong says. "You can put them down, peel them up, put them down. Really ingenious."

Afterward, Adelaide, leaving the scissors behind, reclaims the poker, takes Jason by the hand, and proceeds out the front door to the car. Zora is behind the wheel, and while the family is debating whether she should drive, they spot Umbrae ahead, and Adelaide and Jason get into the car. Gabe instructs her to back up, but instead, Zora accelerates and races forward.

Toward herself.

Only one can survive.

PREVIOUS SPREAD: Filming Kitty's final moments.
TOP: Dahlia performs her own version of cosmetic surgery. **ABOVE:** Josh Tyler's flare gun.

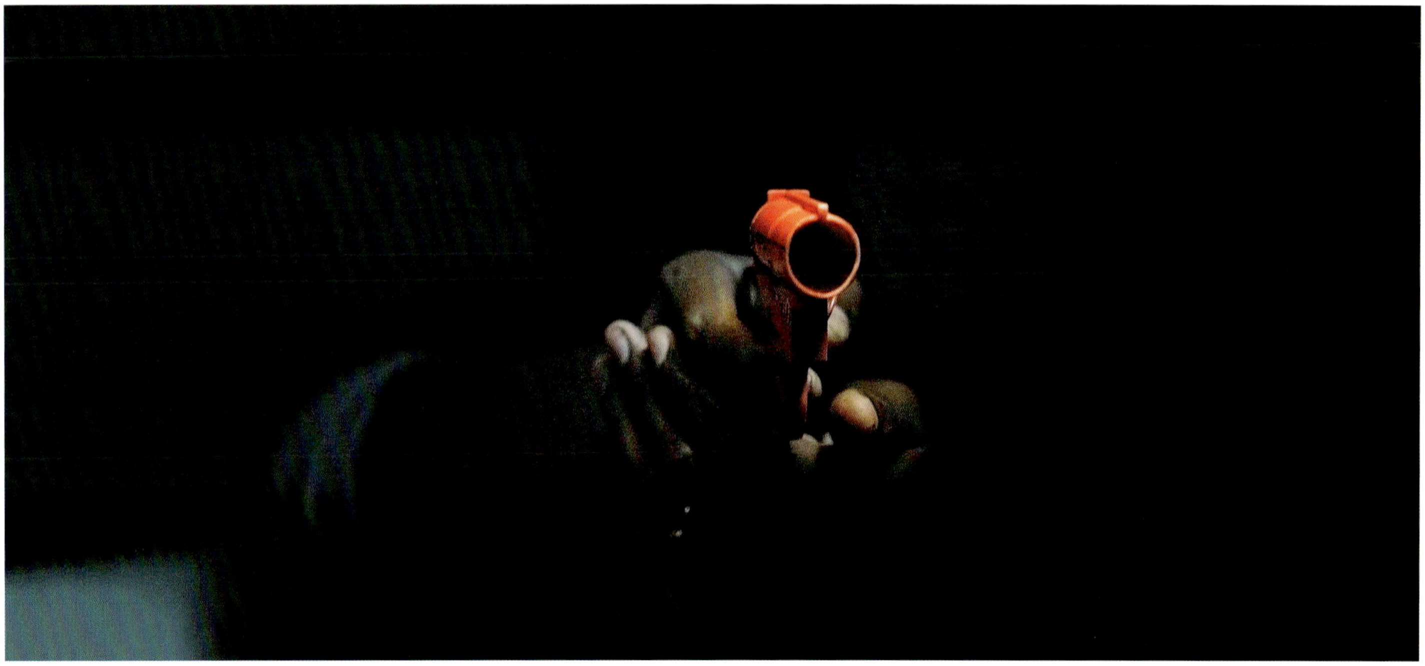

TOP: Jason and Zora find Josh and Kitty's dead bodies.
ABOVE: Gabe uses Josh's "essential" flare gun in his showdown with Tex.

CHAPTER 10

IF IT WEREN'T FOR YOU

After driving through the woods at breakneck speed with the shadow on the hood of the Tylers' car, Zora gets the best of her doppelgänger by slamming on the brakes. The sudden stop sends Umbrae into a nearby tree. Adelaide takes the poker and exits the car, acting on a maternal instinct to see if the "bad" teen is all right. Umbrae is still alive—grunting, gasping, panting, laughing. Adelaide attempts to calm her down, and within a few moments, the breathing slows to a stop.

Adelaide gets behind the wheel of the car and, with tears in her eyes, starts driving her family to safety. Once day breaks, they pass evidence that the Untethering continued throughout the night. People are dead in cars and in the street, clear victims of brutal murders. As the Wilsons drive alongside the Santa Cruz boardwalk, a car engulfed in flames blocks their path. It's *their* own car, which they believed they had left behind at their home.

Pluto, it seems, is responsible. He appears in front of the car, snapping his fingers in front of the Wilsons. The matriarch leaves the vehicle, poker in hand, and approaches Pluto. She reaches out her hand, but instead of taking hers, he lifts his mask to expose his scar, looks at Jason inside the car, and smiles.

"It's a trap," Jason says confidently as he lowers his werewolf mask. "Get out!"

As Gabe, Zora, and Jason run out of the car, Adelaide notices a trail of gasoline leading to the Tylers' vehicle. Pluto has a match, but before he strikes it, Jason extends his arms at his sides and begins walking backward. His doppelgänger follows suit. The two are fully connected in this moment, with Jason walking back from the car and Pluto stepping closer to the fiery vehicle. Adelaide pleads for Pluto to stop, but he defies her. Like the car, he goes up in flames.

OPPOSITE: Red's ballet tutu.
ABOVE: Zora and Gabe share a tender moment among the carnage.

Jason backs up until he is adjacent to a dark-red SUV. Unbeknownst to him, Red is hiding in plain sight—once again, a spider patiently waiting for her prey. She grabs him and runs. Within moments, Adelaide follows them.

Adelaide arrives at the boardwalk. It's a ghost town, with dead bodies strewn about. But there is one sign of life: On the beach, extending from the sand into the Pacific Ocean, there's a line of people in red coveralls. One of the Tethered in the line is the man who once held the cardboard sign. Two pairs of vertical lines representing 11:11 are painted on his forehead in blood.

Determined as ever, Adelaide walks into Merlin's Forest. Despite the rebranding, the interior is the same. Our heroine moves through the faux forest deftly. It isn't just that she's been here before; she seems to be an expert in navigating through the web. She proceeds until she finds the exact spot where she first saw her doppelgänger in 1986. She can remember what her own surprised face looks like, and after pausing for a beat to stiffen her spine, she presses on the hidden door that leads to the world below.

She descends several flights of stairs, through a series of hallways, tunnels, and doors, before arriving at an escalator. The lighting bathes the frame in a golden hue, creating an image eerily reminiscent of the now-infamous image of the escalator ride Donald Trump took to announce his bid for the presidency in 2015. But Adelaide Wilson's journey is leading not to the lobby of Manhattan's lavish Trump Tower, but deeper into the dim, spare, institutional tunnels that house the Tethered—the destitute, forgotten class of Americans.

Adelaide arrives in the Underpass, an elaborate set designed by Ruth De Jong and her team. De Jong spent several days researching underground living communities and bunkers, and along with Peele, she devised a plan to bring the world of the Tethered to life.

"Originally, it was red brick, but we had discussions with Kym Barrett, and we talked about color palettes and textures and surfaces, and we looked at North Korean architecture and 1980s shopping malls," De Jong says. "All of that sort of collided in the final design. There was some really beautiful imagery out of North Korea that inspired me: tile floors, concrete square walls, and all very muted beige tones."

TOP: Adelaide descends deeper into the Underpass.
BELOW: The poker, Adelaide's main method of defense.

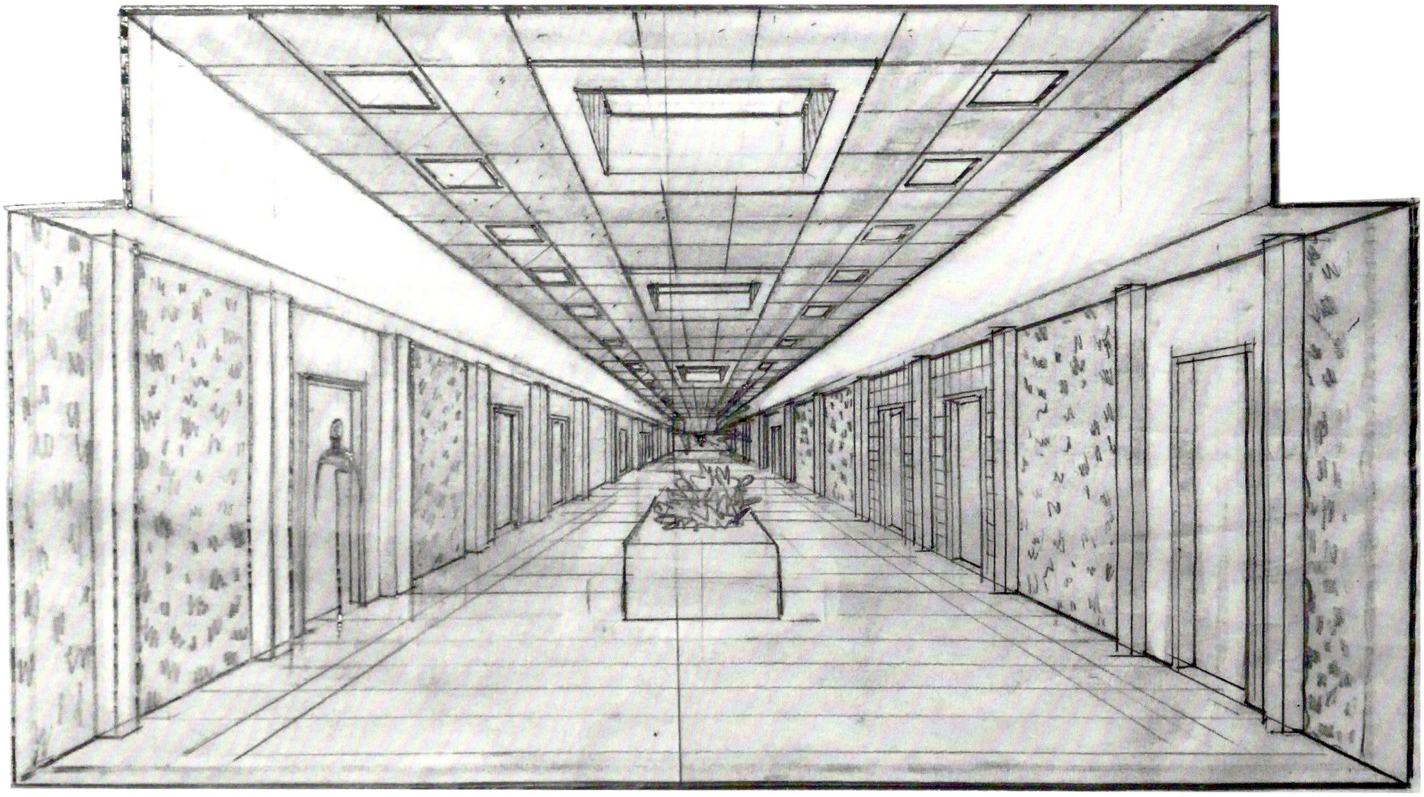

TOP: The schematic for the Underpass Hall corridor set.
ABOVE: The finished Underpass Hall corridor set.

WILSON FAMILY
VERSUS
PLUTO

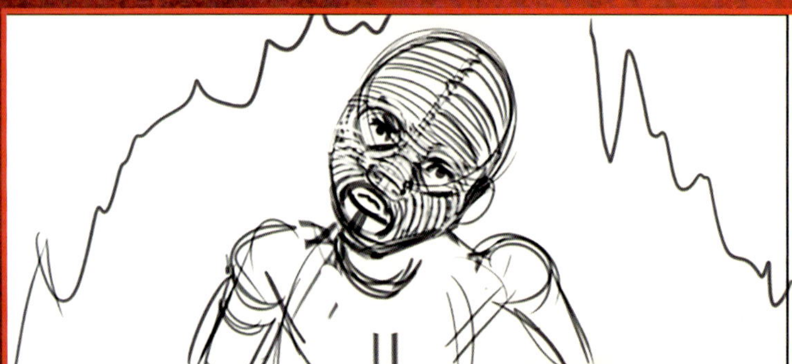

P
A
P
P
J

"Jason and Pluto have a heightened sense of awareness of each other. I thought of Jason as being on the spectrum and that his way of looking at the world somehow affords him a little bit more of a peek at this notion that there is a wrong alignment in the synchronicity of things and that there is this other, and that when they meet each other, they're closer and more curious and open to each other's existence than the other members of the family."

—JORDAN PEELE

"Jordan and I channeled a range of flesh tones that just felt very disturbing," she continues. "We used a lot of squares and a lot of lines that repeated themselves in all of the rooms and all of the architecture. It created this very uncomfortable space."

The Underpass was the largest and most complex build of the shoot, but despite the challenges of constructing the massive set on a Universal Studios soundstage, De Jong was thankful for the opportunity. "Our executive producer, Daniel Lupi, he and I go way back to *There Will Be Blood*," De Jong says. "He enabled us to build a much larger underworld than we had originally planned. I think we were able to go over a hundred feet long. From the get-go, I was like, 'Daniel, I do not have the budget to build this underworld,' and he said, 'No, no, no, Ruth. Do not worry.'"

"He worked it out," she continues. "We were a small but mighty film, shooting between LA and Santa Cruz, but I think we actually got to build everything we wanted to."

The Underpass build was challenging in large part because of the multiple rooms. Within the narrative of the film, the Tethered are relegated to this underground lair day and night, which requires the space to be enormous. Even with De Jong's expanded budget, a number of cinematic tricks were used to make the Underpass appear vast on screen. "The hallway was designed in a modular way, with some of the walls on rollers, so that the team could move and configure them however they wanted," visual-effects supervisor Grady Cofer says. "They could line it up so that the hallway ended at a green screen, and then we could extend digitally. That allowed us to create a kind of labyrinth—this endless, complicated maze—and we could adjust it on the fly depending on what we wanted the environment to be."

While Cofer and his team at ILM contributed 238 visual-effects shots to *Us*, all the rabbits in the Underpass were real. "We started talking about digital rabbit duplication, or creating [computer-generated] rabbits, just throwing ideas out there," he says. "But Jordan decided to get hundreds of rabbits and shot the whole thing in camera."

Rabbits are present throughout most of the film—from the opening credits to Addy's stuffed animal to Zora's clothing and throughout the Tethereds' underground lair. Within the context of the narrative, their importance is explained by Red during the home-invasion sequence: "When the shadow was hungry, he had to eat rabbit raw and bloody."

Interestingly, this bit of information from Red further emphasizes the injustice the Tethered face underground: Humans are incapable of surviving on an exclusive diet of rabbit meat. Even though protein-rich rabbits will leave people feeling full, lean meats lack nutrients necessary for survival, and overconsumption will result in death. Not only did the U.S. government supposedly create the Tethered as a class of have-nots, they also denied them their most basic right as Americans—the ability to pursue life, liberty, and happiness.

Rabbits are also symbols of rebirth. They are animals known for reproducing at a rapid rate—multiplying like rabbits—and are closely connected with Easter, a Christian holiday commemorating the resurrection of Jesus Christ. Their presence throughout *Us* suggests that the Tethered are being given, or are taking, their chance to overtake their aboveground counterparts.

According to Peele, there is another reason he wrote rabbits into the script—they terrify him. "Rabbits are creepy. I've never really been completely comfortable with rabbits," he says. "Most fuzzy, fluffy animals have some kind of a personality. Rabbits have those dead eyes. It's like, when they look at you, it's like they're looking through you or looking past you.

PAGES 104-107: Pluto's face off with the Wilson family.
TOP: One of the Underpass rabbits. **ABOVE:** One of Zora's rabbit t-shirts.

“They’re an animal of duality,” he has also stated. “They’re adorable but they terrify me at the same time. And they got those scissor-like ears that creep me out.”

Adelaide finally finds Red in a classroom. She is using her scissors to create dolls out of red sheets of paper, just like the ones young Addy saw in the Hands Across America commercial in 1986. She’s standing in front of a long chalkboard, filled with stick figures of people, their hands tethered, stretching across its full width. Throughout the room, countless red handprints are splattered on the walls.

As Red attempts to jog Adelaide’s memory of the night the two met in the Shaman’s Vision Quest, we see another flashback: Peele cuts between what occurred at the Santa Cruz boardwalk and how the Tethered would clumsily approximate or translate those actions underground. We see Weyland, the doppelgänger for Russel, Addy’s father, present his daughter with a distorted, bizarre version of the “Thriller” T-shirt.

During a flashback, we see Young Red take Addy’s Hands Across America shirt and hang it in her barracks locker. Over the years, it served as a source of inspiration for what would ultimately become the Untethering.

TOP: Red visually demonstrates The Untethering with paper cutouts.
ABOVE: Young Addy’s Hands Across America shirt hangs in an Underpass locker.

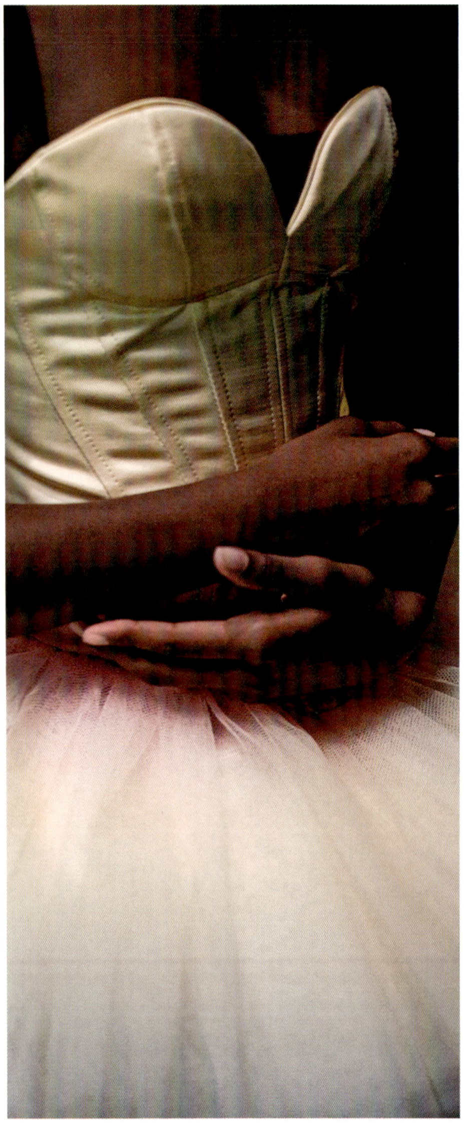

Red's flashbacks bring us to what she describes as "the miracle," the day she saw God. For the first time, we see Adelaide and Red as teenagers, performing the grand pas de deux from *The Nutcracker* ballet.

"In *The Nutcracker*, the character Clara ventures into the land of candy and fantasy that is actually a dark dream realm, so that coincided with some of the themes in the film," *Us* choreographer Madeline Hollander says. "Jordan wanted teen Adelaide to be a dancer who decided to do the grand pas de deux, a dance for two people, as a solo piece. This is essentially impossible and tells us a lot about her personality."

Ashley McKoy played both Adelaide and Red as teenagers, requiring her to learn a reimagined iteration of the well-known duet. "I figured out ways to create different types of balancing that create the illusion of being partnered, or use the walls," Hollander says. "After that we had to figure out how to invert all of that content for a parallel scene—a darker, twisted version of the same choreography.

"I started taking clips from the grand pas de deux and reversing them, just to see what the movement would look like," she continues. "It turns the choreography into impossible movements, because of all the balancing and jumping, and the delicacy of it. Reversing a jump never looks like a landing.

"I visualized it as if teen Adelaide and teen Red were connected by magnets, and teen Red was directly underneath the stage below her," Hollander concludes. "In that situation, teen Red would be dragged around, like a marionette being controlled by a force above her, but she would also have some agency and power of her own. We had to figure out how to balance those opposing forces in the choreography."

The climax of the film occurs when Adelaide and Red have an epic battle. Peele crosscuts between the present day and a flashback, juxtaposing the current fight with the pas de deux that made Red realize she and Addy are special. The sequence is scored to "The Tethered Mix" of "I Got 5 on It," creating not only a narrative payoff but a musical one as well.

PREVIOUS SPREAD: Peele and Red in the Underpass classroom.
ABOVE: Red and Adelaide perform the grand pas de deux from *The Nutcracker* ballet.

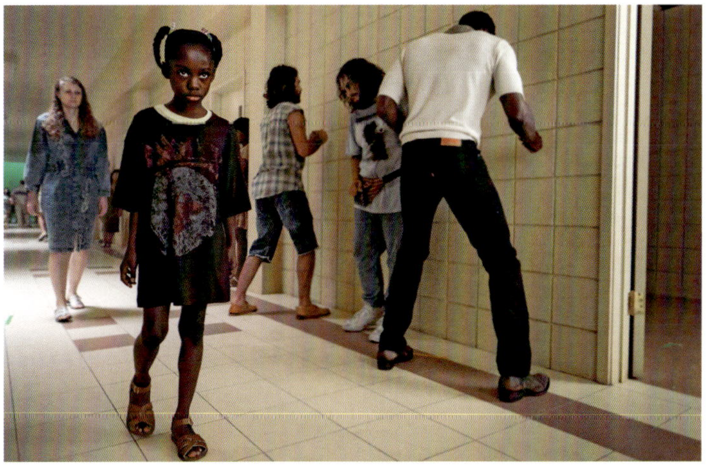

In the end, a bloodied and weakened Adelaide gets the best of her shadow, stabbing her in the gut with the poker. Red faintly whistles "The Itsy-Bitsy Spider" until Adelaide wraps her handcuffed wrists around her doppelgänger's neck. It takes just a few moments for the chain to claim Red's last breath.

Red's neck snaps. Adelaide lets out a primal scream before gnashing her teeth and panting. She looks into Red's dead eyes and begins to chuckle to herself. She grabs the key from around Red's neck and goes to retrieve Jason, who has been hiding in a locker.

They return to ground level and reunite with Gabe and Zora. They've commandeered an ambulance, and with the family unit back together, they ride off toward safety. Adelaide drives with Jason beside her in the passenger seat, white rabbit on his lap.

Our heroine's mind wanders back to her childhood one final time.

She remembers therapy after the incident.

Dance lessons.

The Shaman's Vision Quest.

The hands around her double's throat.

She remembers dragging Addy into the Underpass.

Stealing her "Thriller" shirt.

Tethering her to the bed.

Smiling as she returns to the beach.

She remembers being in the backseat of a strange car.

Beginning a new life.

Stealing an old one.

She remembers.

TOP: Young Addy's doppelganger prepares to leave the Underpass.
ABOVE: Young Addy's doppelganger puts on the Thriller shirt.

She looks at Jason. He stares at the woman he's known all his life. She gives him a wry smile and turns away. He lowers his mask, never averting his gaze.

For the moment, mother and son's true identities are concealed.

As the Wilsons continue to drive toward what they hope will be safety, Peele takes his audience out of their vehicle. We see the ambulance moving down the road from the perspective of a helicopter. The distance makes the vehicle appear small, no bigger than Jason's toy ambulance.

The Wilsons do not know it, but in the distance, thousands of hands have interconnected across the American terrain. Red may be dead, but her mission—the shared mission of the Tethered—lives on.

ABOVE: Adelaide and Jason exchange knowing looks.

TOP: The Tethered stretch their hands across America.
ABOVE: Adelaide's paper dolls, tethered together.
FOLLOWING SPREAD: Peele looks on at the line of Tethered.

EPILOGUE

IT'S US

Immediately upon its March 2019 release in the United States, *Us* became one of the most critically and commercially successful horror films of all time.

In one of the many stellar reviews of the film, Monica Castillo of *RogerEbert.com* wrote that "*Us* is another thrilling exploration of the past and oppression this country is still too afraid to bring up. Peele wants us to talk, and he's given audiences the material to think, to feel our way through some of the darker sides of the human condition and the American experience."

Even more so than giving audiences a thrilling and entertaining experience while watching the film, Peele agrees that what occurs after the ending credits—the talking and thinking—is a significant reason why he creates films.

"The most rewarding part for me is to see people engaged in conversation in things I'm interested in," he says. "And I'm always trying to point my commentary at things that I feel like deserve conversation. I love that."

Even before the film's opening, journalists and content creators took to the internet to share theories, point out Easter eggs, and analyze every moment of *Us* they could get their eyes on. The search for deeper meaning has become an important part of the film's legacy, with fans of the film hungry to learn more while also satisfied with embracing the movie's mystery.

With *Us*, Peele created a timeless film—for better or for worse.

OPPOSITE: The Tethered version of Young Addy's Thriller t-shirt.
ABOVE: One of The Tethered in the Underpass.

No one could have predicted that almost a year to the day after *Us* was released, America's longstanding issues with inequity would be on full display. A pandemic response that quickly became politicized, followed later that year by a nationwide racial uprising and a tumultuous presidential election—which culminated in an insurrection attempt at the US Capitol—caught the world by surprise. It was a defining moment in the country's history, and in some ways, our collective response to what occurred in 2020—eerily, yet another number of duality—was the culmination of fissures that had existed just below the surface for years.

It is fitting that in *Us*, Peele invited his audience to take stock of their contributions to systems of oppression and injustice. As millions of Americans were forced "underground" while tethered to their homes, looking back at themselves while videoconferencing with friends, family, and colleagues, there was no better opportunity for both literal and metaphorical self-reflection.

"Why is seeing yourself so scary? I think no one really wants to look at their faults, their guilt, their demons," Peele says. "We all want to look elsewhere.

"I would have to say I've lived a privileged life of an American," he adds. "I grew up middle class, had an education. I've always been fed, I've always had shoes, and I've neglected what that privilege means in terms of the people who have suffered and continue to suffer. We're connected to other people. Somebody made these shoes.

"That was the part of the message that I wanted to then apply to the 'US' of it—the United States," he concludes. "We have an ability to cover up what is uncomfortable for us to face about ourselves."

Five years after the film's release, we are still grappling with who gets to be seen and counted as an American, and experiencing the horrors that arise when we find our ourselves face to face with those who fail to see the full humanity in others.

ABOVE: Adelaide comes face to face with her counterpart in the Wilson sitting room.

The enemy is within—and it's us.

Given that the United States has recommitted to a political movement many in the country had hoped would be a short-lived aberration, the themes and messages of *Us* are all the more relevant—more so than they were during the time of its release. Though we are the United States, in many ways, there are two Americas. It may seem that each side has its own reality, and may even consider themselves to be have-nots, but it is easy to forget that we are together in the house of mirrors: What we see isn't always real. There are distortions and wrong ways, especially along the path to find oneself.

"I didn't set out to make a movie about a post-Trump America," Peele says, "but it's not an accident. My fears were surrounding this sense of us as a collective. Our demons."

"Certainly I, at a certain point, decided to use United States imagery," he continues. "From whether it's the genocide of the Native American people, Black Lives Matter, or our xenophobia and privilege, but however you define 'us,' in order for us to have 'us,' there's got to be a 'them.'"

"And I think that's, in its core, what this movie is about," he concludes. "We will value our own, however we see it, more than we'll value the other."

ABOVE: Jason and Zora in the Tyler home.

WILSON FAMILY
VERSUS
UMBRAE

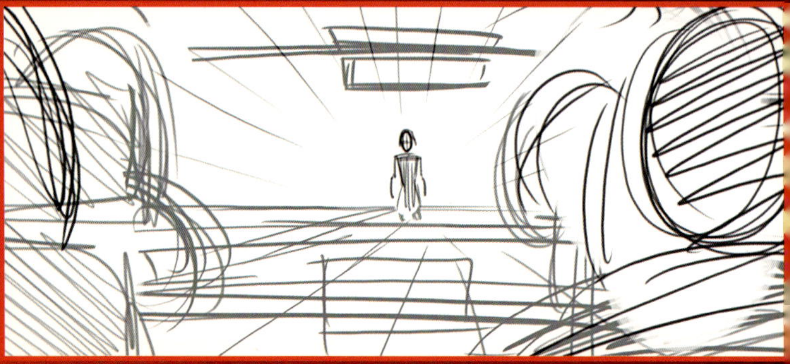

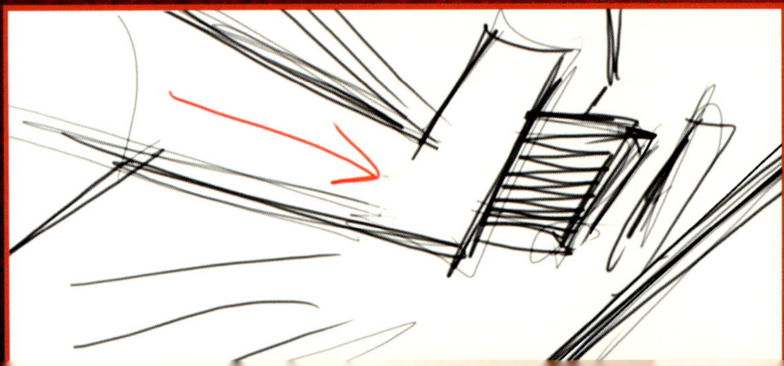

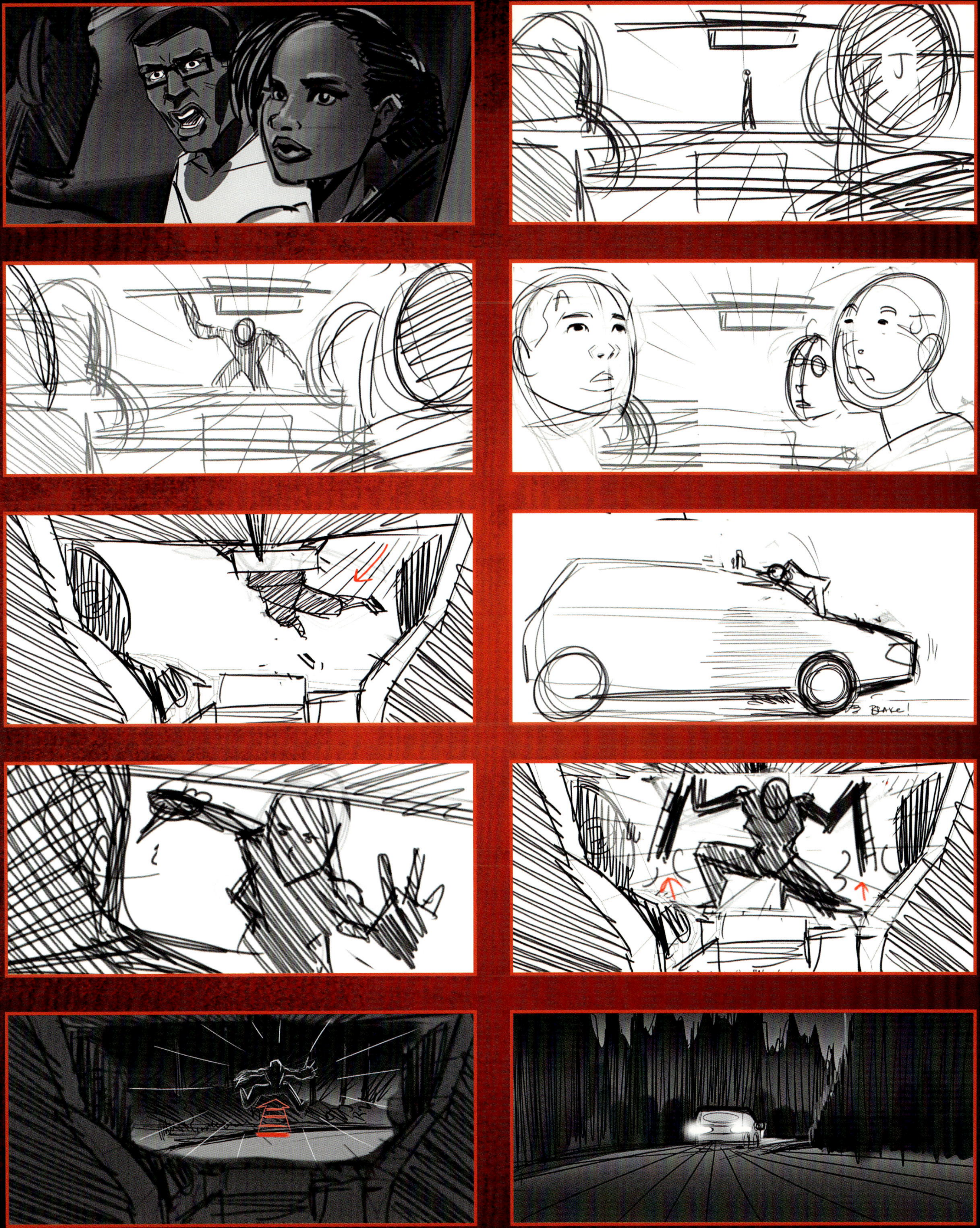
BRAKE!

"The theme of synchronicity arose early, and the idea came from an existential sense that something was off in the country and that the natural state of things is in misalignment. And when they line up, it's a sign that something unnatural is happening, something more of design than nature."

—JORDAN PEELE

INSIGHT EDITIONS

PO Box 3088
San Rafael, CA 94912
www.insighteditions.com

Find us on Facebook: www.facebook.com/InsightEditions
Follow us on Instagram: @insighteditions

ISBN: 979-8-8866-3664-2

Publisher: Raoul Goff

SVP, Group Publisher: Vanessa Lopez

VP, Creative: Chrissy Kwasnik

VP, Manufacturing: Alix Nicholaeff

Editorial Director: Lia Brown

Art Director: Matt Girard

Designer: Allister Fein

Senior Editor: Sarah Southard

Editorial Assistant: Alecsander Zapata

Executive Managing Editor: Maria Spano

Senior Production Manager: Greg Steffen

Strategic Production Planner: Lina s Palma-Temena

Cover design by La Boca.

ROOTS of PEACE REPLANTED PAPER

Insight Editions, in association with Roots of Peace, will plant two trees for each tree used in the manufacturing of this book. Roots of Peace is an internationally renowned humanitarian organization dedicated to eradicating land mines worldwide and converting war-torn lands into productive farms and wildlife habitats. Roots of Peace will plant two million fruit and nut trees in Afghanistan and provide farmers there with the skills and support necessary for sustainable land use.

Manufactured in China by Insight Editions

10 9 8 7 6 5 4 3 2 1

PAGES 122–123: Storyboards for Umbrae's showdown with the Wilson family.
PAGES 124–125: Peele in the Underpass.
PREVIOUS: Pluto outside the Wilson house.

ACKNOWLEDGMENTS

After just a few minutes into *Get Out*, Jordan Peele had already become one of my all-time favorite writer-directors. I have always been drawn to stories that blended social commentary with science fiction, like *The Twilight Zone* and *Planet of the Apes*, and Peele's work is a spiritual successor to those classics, made even more impactful that he is a Black American who masterfully and entertainingly speaks to our experience.

I couldn't wait to see what he would come up with next, and *Us* exceeded my expectations. The film intrigued me from the first trailer through multiple rewatches and the writing of this book. It was an honor to explore this film, and the artistry of Jordan Peele and his collaborators, in this book.

To Jordan Peele, Ian Cooper, Hewot Getachew, Alex Kim, Daniel Larson, Ethan Soo, and the entire team at Monkeypaw, I cannot thank you enough for entrusting me and for all the behind-the-scenes work you did on this project. Also, just thank you for telling stories that inspire me as a writer and captivate me as a viewer and reader. I love your work.

To the team at Universal—Mariana Galvez, Kelsey Parrotte, Megan Startz, Julie Berk, Shelby Butler-Santiel, Britt Shotts, and Connie Shao—thank you for your assistance with seeing this project to fruition. This couldn't have been done without you.

To the team at Insight Editions—Vanessa Lopez, Sarah Southard, Tim Pilcher, Alecsander Zapata, Allister Fein, and Matt Girard—thank you for once again granting me the opportunity to work with you. I am always in awe of the finished products you put out.

Special thanks to Peter Steinberg, my amazing agent, Harry Sherer, and everyone at UTA for everything, as well as Jen Hale, Kate Napolitano, Chris Prince, and Anna Michels, my editors on past projects. Everything I write is better because of everything I've written.

This book is extra special because of the contributions of those who took time to speak with me and, in some cases, open up their archives. I offer the greatest thanks to the following people for their time and access: Jordan Peele, Michael Abels, Kym Barrett, Ian Cooper, Ruth De Jong, and Eric Yamamoto—and thanks to their managers, agents, and assistants who helped facilitate our interviews.

Thanks to my friends and family, with special shout outs to my wife, Johanna Calle, my parents, Bernadette and Curtis, and my brother, Curtis Gaines III. Thank you for always being there.
I love you.

—Caseen Gaines

caseen@caseengaines.com
www.caseengaines.com
Social Media: @caseengaines